Healing the Cause

A PATH OF FORGIVENESS

D0063033

Healing the Cause

A PATH OF FORGIVENESS

Michael Dawson

Findhorn Press

British Library Cataloguing-in-Publication Data. A catalogue
record for this book is available from the British Library.

Portions from *A Course in Miracles* © 1975, *Psychotherapy: Purpose, Process and Practice* © 1976, *The Song Of Prayer* © 1978,
reprinted by permission of the Foundation for Inner Peace, Inc.,
P.O. Box 1104, Glen Ellen, California 95442, USA.

The quotation from *A Treatise on the Seven Rays, Vol IV, Esoteric
Healing* by Alice A. Bailey is used by permission of the Lucis
Trust.

The quotation from *Jesus, Teacher and Healer* by White Eagle is
used by permission of The White Eagle Lodge.

The ideas represented herein are the personal interpretation
and understanding of the author and are not necessarily
endorsed by the copyright holder for *A Course in Miracles*.

The quotations on the back cover are from *A Course in Miracles*
Text page 15/18 and the Manual for Teachers page 16/17
respectively.

Cover painting by Karin Werner
Author photograph by Findhorn Foundation Visual Arts
Cover design and diagrams by Posthouse Printing
Layout and setting in Palatino by Findhorn Press
Printed and bound by Cromwell Press Ltd,
Melksham, England

Published by Findhorn Press, The Park, Findhorn,
Forres IV36 OTZ, Moray, Scotland

A Course in Miracles has been the inspiration for this book. What I have written is my own interpretation of some of the principles in the Course and, as such, it cannot match the depth and purity of the original teaching. If you find my book of interest I would encourage you to study the Course's teaching, for which there can be no substitute.

For Salice who has helped me so much and for Kenneth Wapnick who has guided my path of understanding.

Contents

Author's Note

The thought system in *A Course in Miracles* is the foundation for this book. I first started to read the Course in the early 1980s, and once I completed it I put it aside. One day I received through the mail two introductory books on the Course — *A Talk Given On A Course in Miracles* and *Christian Psychology in A Course in Miracles* — both written by Dr Kenneth Wapnick. To this day, I do not know who sent them. Reading the books gave me considerable new insights into the Course's thought system and this encouraged me to continue studying the Course. Since that time I have received great help from Kenneth Wapnick's books and tapes, as well as his personal help in the production of this book. His review of its outline and his insightful comments on the first draft produced major changes in the finished book. I find Ken's teaching models and ideas excellent in putting across a thought system that is initially difficult to understand. Over the years I have absorbed many of Ken's ideas and inevitably some of them are reflected in this book, especially in Chapters Three and Four.

I am also indebted to my wife Salice, a fellow student of the Course, who has been a constant source of help and encouragement throughout the planning and writing of this book. Salice has literally scrutinised every word and given invaluable comments on style and content, as well as typing the entire manuscript.

The combination of Salice's and Ken's advice guaranteed that I wrote a much better book than if I had followed through on my original ideas. At times my ego felt quite threatened by their combined attention. However, I know the main purpose of writing this book is to help me move closer to the reality of spirit and their astute feedback has served me in this purpose.

I also wish to give thanks to Caroline Myss for her thoughtful review of the outline of the book and her encouragement to get it published.

Lastly I would like to thank the following people who read the manuscript and offered me their support and suggestions — Charles Frizell, David Pashby, Sandra Kramer and Lori Sunshine.

Reference Notation System

The following references have been used in this book for quotations taken from *A Course in Miracles* and two related pamphlets:

Text (T)
Workbook (W)
Manual for Teachers (M)
Psychotherapy: Purpose, Process and Practice (P)
The Song of Prayer (S)

The Course and the two pamphlets are now in their Second Edition with different page numbering. The first reference after the quotation will be one of the above letters followed by the page number for the First Edition. Then comes a semi colon, followed by notations that locate the reference in the Second Edition. Please see page 158 for an explanation and examples of this.

Although the case histories in this book are true, the clients' names and other identifying features have been changed to ensure privacy.

I have used male pronouns throughout this book and I apologise to anyone who finds this practice offensive. I have done so to conform to the rules of grammar and avoid the constant clumsiness of 'he or she', 'himself or herself', 'his or her' etc. No inequality between the sexes is in any way intended.

Nothing real can be threatened.
Nothing unreal exists.
Herein lies the peace of God

from *A Course in Miracles* (Intro, Text)

Chapter One

Introduction

*It is your thoughts alone that cause you pain. Nothing exter-
nal to your mind can hurt or injure you in any way. There is
no cause beyond yourself that can reach down and bring oppres-
sion. No one but yourself affects you. There is nothing in the
world that has the power to make you ill or sad, or weak or frail.
But it is you who have the power to dominate all things you see
by merely recognising what you are.*

from *A Course in Miracles* (W351; W-pI.190.5:1-6)[1]

Symptom Relief Versus Healing

*False healing can indeed remove a form of pain and sick-
ness. But the cause remains, and will not lack effects.*

(S16; S-3.II.1:4-5)

'I've had this headache for three days and nights. Can you
help me?' Joan was the mother of a friend of mine and
had heard I was quite good at relieving headaches
through giving massage. 'I've consulted two doctors but
have not received any relief. Unless I keep my head
upright, I feel nauseous as well.' After listening to the
severity of the symptoms, I felt my simple head massage
technique would be of little value in this case. However,
I said I would do my best and asked her to lie down and
relax. To help centre and relax myself, I laid my hands
gently on her head for about a minute. When I felt more
at peace, I started the first massage strokes on her scalp.
Almost immediately Joan said, 'Thank you, the pain has

[1] Please see page 9 for an explanation of page and line references to
A Course in Miracles.

all gone!' But it can't have, I thought, I have hardly started yet!

This experience had a profound effect on me. What was going on here? I started to read about spiritual healing and the laying on of hands. It was pleasing to think I might have special powers or energies which could help others. My friends began to turn to me to help them with their aches and pains and I was happy to try and help. On most occasions it was possible to reduce or eliminate their pains.

Whilst visiting a friend, I was introduced to his flat-mate, Peter. He suffered from life-long lower back pain. On hearing that I gave healing, he asked me for a session. As I worked with him, he reported that the pain was moving out of his spine and into his right buttock. From there the pain travelled to his right leg and finally left his body via his foot. The whole process took about ten minutes. He was free of pain for the rest of the day. The following morning, the back pain had returned to its normal level.

I had noticed this return of symptoms on other occasions — headaches, back pains and other complaints had been cured for a while and had then returned. This was not always the case but had happened often enough to arouse my curiosity. It reminded me of people who had chronic pain which could be relieved by medication; however, the pain would return the moment the effect of the medicine wore off. Were my hands simply a form of aspirin to be taken regularly? And if so, was I doing the best I could for my clients? Why did the pain return sometimes? What was the causative level of the problem? I began to read widely on this subject, especially in the field of psychosomatic medicine.

The link between the mind and the body began to assume a major importance in my research. As long ago as 500 BC Socrates had said, 'There is no illness of the body apart from the mind.' Even Louis Pasteur, the father of antibiotics, stated 'It is not the bacteria, it is the terrain.' My study of spiritual healing took me into the area of channelled books. Here I found deep sources of wisdom and inspiration. I became a member of the Arcane School which was started by Alice A. Bailey. Over a number of years she had telepathically received some 18 volumes of esoteric teachings, including the book *A Treatise on the Seven Rays, Vol IV, Esoteric Healing*. In here I read:

> *The basic law underlying all occult healing, may be stated as follows: All disease is the result of inhibited soul life, and that is true of all forms in all kingdoms. The art of the healer consists in releasing the soul, so that its life can flow through the aggregate of organisms which constitute any particular form.*

This struck a chord within me which was reinforced by the study of the White Eagle literature. White Eagle was the spirit guide of a woman called Grace Cooke. In *Jesus Teacher and Healer* by White Eagle, I found the following statement:

> *When the body is sick, it is in some way lacking the light. All disease will in due time be traced to this.*

Intuitively I felt I had come across the key I needed to understand the causative level of disease. I saw that the condition of the body depends on the state of the mind. If we use the body in a loveless fashion, it starts to break down and disintegrate. If we use it as a tool of loving communication, it will remain healthy and serve us well.

I now realised that if my clients wanted a healing that lasted, they would need to participate in the healing session. They would have to be willing to go deeper than their bodily symptoms and learn to heal some dark spot in their minds, of which the bodily condition was just a shadow. I was no longer satisfied in offering my hands as 'aspirins' to be taken twice a week by clients until they were well. What seemed important now was to provide a supportive and non-judgemental presence which would facilitate my clients' changing their minds about some issue in their life. Later, I would realise that I was trying to aid them in their process of forgiveness.

At about this time I visited an international spiritual community in the north of Scotland called the Findhorn Foundation. It was here that I discovered a book that was to change the direction of my life.

A Course in Miracles

One day, after finishing my lunch in the Community Centre at the Foundation, I visited the Phoenix Craft and Book Shop. In the window were displayed the three volumes of a book entitled *A Course in Miracles*. The title did not appeal to me very much but I was drawn to inspecting them. I picked up the largest volume called the 'Text', opened it at random and read a paragraph. I cannot remember what I read, but I do recall its impact. It was like receiving a shock and it made a deep impression upon me. The book seemed to have no author, just the name of the publishers — the Foundation for Inner Peace, USA. The second largest of the three volumes was called 'Workbook for Students' and contained 365 lessons designed to apply the theoretical foundation described in the Text on a practical level in our everyday lives. The smallest volume was entitled 'Manual for Teachers' and contained summaries of the Course's principal themes in a question and answer format.

The following day I was drawn back to this window display, whereupon I again read at random from the three books. I kept this up for two weeks until I had to return to London. The memory of the impact of the book stayed with me and I wrote to the Phoenix Bookshop for a copy. I soon discovered that I had come across another channelled book which would deeply affect my approach to healing myself and others.

How *A Course in Miracles* Came

The way the Course came to be written illustrates very well the principles to be found within its pages. In 1957 William Thetford, a professor of medical psychology, was made Director of the Psychology Department at the Columbia-Presbyterian Medical Center in New York City. The following year he appointed Helen Schucman, an associate professor of medical psychology, to head a research project. Although they worked well together professionally, their personal and departmental relationships were marked with much criticism, anger and blame. Each felt the other to be the cause of their unhappiness.

During 1965 Bill said to Helen that there had to be 'another way' to relate to each other and within and between departments. Helen agreed with him and said she would help him to find it. This is an example of what the Course would call 'a holy instant', where instead of holding on to a grievance, forgiveness is chosen instead. This shift of perception is what the Course calls a miracle.

The moment of joining between them was the moment that the Course was born. Helen soon began to experience dreams, visions and psychic experiences which she found very disturbing to her logical, rational and scientifically-oriented mind. Bill was very supportive towards her and managed to convince her she was not going mad.

During the October of 1965 Helen 'heard' in her mind the words 'This is a Course in Miracles. Please take notes.' In desperation she rang Bill who tried to placate her and suggested she take down this inner dictation and bring it to the office the following day. He told Helen that if it was found to be nonsense, they could simply discard it and no one need ever know anything about it.

However, it soon became clear that the Course contained profound teachings and they could not easily dismiss it. For the next seven years, Helen continued to receive this inner dictation which she wrote down in shorthand. She said it was like having a tape recorder in her mind which she could start and stop at will, even in mid-sentence. Bill continued to support and encourage Helen in this process and would daily type the notes as Helen read them from her shorthand notebook.

The Course comes from Jesus, with much of it written in the first person. Several references are made to his life 2,000 years ago, especially with regard to his crucifixion which he describes in a very different light to what we have been taught to believe. Helen was shocked to realise who the source of this material was. At this time of her life she posed as an atheist. She had sought to find God in her early years but felt she had failed. She had retained an anger against a deity whom she felt had not made the same effort towards her. Her ambivalence towards God now extended to Jesus, with whom she maintained a love/hate relationship for the rest of her life. In the Course, Jesus tells us he understands that many of us experience difficulty in relating to him and that we need not believe he is the author of the Course to benefit from his words. (see M84; C-5.6)

The Course has been published as it was received except for the removal of material personal to Helen and Bill. The Text was received in one block and needed editing in the form of inserting chapter and section headings, punctuation, paragraphing and capitalisation. They were helped in this work by Dr Kenneth Wapnick, a clinical psychologist. Ken tells the whole fascinating story of how *A Course in Miracles* was born in his book *Absence from Felicity — The Story of Helen Schucman and Her Scribing of A Course in Miracles*, published by the Foundation for A Course in Miracles.[2] Bill looked upon his work with Helen as a 'sacred trust'. The Course was the answer to their joint need for 'another way' of relating.

Two further channelled writings came through Helen from Jesus in the form of pamphlets. The first was completed in 1975, three years after the Course was written. It is entitled *Psychotherapy: Purpose, Process and Practice* and is a summary of the Course's teachings on healing as applied to the profession of psychotherapy. In 1977 Helen channelled *The Song of Prayer*. This was in response to questions Ken had raised about the correct use of prayer. It is a poetic summary of prayer, forgiveness and healing.

After Helen's death in 1981, a book of her inspired poetry was published, entitled *The Gifts of God*.

What the Course Is

Much of the material in this book is based upon my understanding of some of the principles of the Course. I have included below some introductory material about what the Course says.

It is a book about how to heal our minds, for this is where the source of all our physical and psychological suffering lies. The aim of the Course is for us to achieve a state of inner peace, a quiet joy, no matter what we are doing, who we are with, or where we may be. It does this by teaching us a new way of looking at the world. This change of perception is the miracle — hence the title of the book.

The Course teaches that everything in this world can be used as a mirror to what we believe. Our relationships are the most powerful of all our mirrors. By relationships I mean all forms: lovers, parent and child, therapist and client, employer and employee, friends, etc. A relationship

---

[2] Please see the Appendix for details of Kenneth Wapnick's books about the Course and the Foundation for A Course in Miracles which he directs with his wife Gloria.

is an extremely powerful way of bringing into our awareness what needs to be healed within our mind. The Course teaches that through forgiveness and turning within for help, we can undo all the guilt we carry. This guilt originates from the false belief in our unconscious mind that we have willed to separate ourself from God, and have succeeded in this attempt. Chapter 2 will explore this theme more fully. Guilt is the term the Course uses to describe our self-hate, feelings of inferiority, lack of self-worth and all the negative beliefs we have about ourself. As we learn to undo our guilt, the memory of God's love for us will return to our mind. When we re-experience the unconditional love of God, everything in this world will lose its appeal, including our identification with our body. (See Figure 1.1)

The Course is a unique blend of modern psychology, radical metaphysics and deep spiritual truths. Much of the psychology is derived from Sigmund Freud's teachings on our ego defence mechanisms of denial and projection and will be explained further in Chapter 3. The three volumes comprising the Course are a lifetime study requiring much re-reading to benefit from the depths of its teachings. The metaphysics of the Course have many parallels with some Eastern philosophies and religions.[3] There are over 700 references to the Bible, and Jesus often reinterprets these biblical sayings. Many Christian terms are used in the Course but with entirely different meanings. Jesus stresses that we are not guilty, sinful creatures who need to atone through sacrifice and suffering. Instead, he gives us the inspiring message that we are guiltless, sinless creations of God who have fallen asleep in Heaven. In our collective dream, we have forgotten the abstract eternal beauty of our real nature and believe we

[3] See *Be As You Are — The Teachings of Sri Ramana Maharshi*. Editor David Godman, Arkana Publications.

'The World I See Holds Nothing that I Want.'
(Title of Lesson 128)

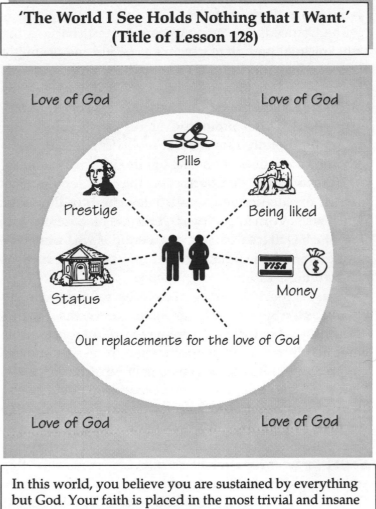

Love of God   Love of God

Pills

Prestige   Being liked

Status   Money

Our replacements for the love of God

Love of God   Love of God

In this world, you believe you are sustained by everything but God. Your faith is placed in the most trivial and insane symbols; pills, money, 'protective' clothing, influence, prestige, being liked, knowing the 'right' people, and an endless list of forms of nothingness that you endow with magical powers. All these things are your replacements for the Love of God. All these things are cherished to ensure a body identification. They are songs of praise to the ego. Do not put your faith in the worthless. It will not sustain you. Only the Love of God will protect you in all circumstances. W79; W-pI.50.1:2-3, 2, 3:1

Fig 1.1

are bodies in a world of form.

The Course is not trying to convince us that it is the only spiritual path. It states that it is but one of 'many thousands' of spiritual paths and that other teachers with different symbols are also needed. (M3; M-1.4:1-2) Jesus often says that the message of his Course is simple. However, when we first start to study it, it does not appear that way to most of us. This is because the Course's thought system is completely opposite to our ego's way of looking at the world. The Course uses the term 'ego'— as is also the practice in the East — to describe our 'little self' which we have made to try and take the place of our real Self which God created. Our ego identifies with our body whilst our Self (or Christ nature) knows only the truth of our formless, spiritual magnificence.

Jesus stresses that all God's children, referred to in the Course as the Son, Sonship or Christ, were created equal. Thus Jesus is not especially favoured in God's eyes but is equal to all of us. He simply awoke to his true reality before us and seeks to help us regain what we have forgotten. In later chapters I will expand on some of the Course's teachings, especially with regard to healing our mind.

The Text in particular seems hard to grasp and the practice of forgiveness equally as difficult. Because of this some people tend only to read the Workbook. However, there is much material in the Text, especially with regard to relationships, which is not found in the Workbook. The Text forms the theoretical foundation of the Workbook. It becomes very easy to misunderstand the Workbook and read its message out of context without a knowledge of the theoretical framework of the Course which is found in the Text. On the other hand, to study the Text but not apply it through the Workbook lessons is to end up with an ungrounded and abstract view of the Course. Yet, with time, the message of the Course does become simple, although never easy to apply. Victim consciousness is ingrained in our psyches and the desire to blame others for our unhappiness is universal. To read in the Course (see first quotation on page 13) that no one can take away our peace, only ourselves, is a difficult message to accept, but one which will eventually lead us to happiness.

Health is Inner Peace . . . Health is the result of relinquishing all attempts to use the body lovelessly.
(T15; T-2.I.5:11; T146; T-8.VIII.9:9)

After my first visit to the Findhorn Foundation, I returned the following year and took part in a healing workshop. During this period I said 'yes' to working more deeply with healing. I did not realise until much later that this was the path I had chosen to help heal myself. Most of the people at the Foundation believe that their thinking at least contributes to their disease. This allowed me to help my clients reach deeper levels in their mind where a lack of forgiveness lay and gave them the opportunity to change their mind about some painful issue. If my client could achieve forgiveness, his sense of guilt would disappear and its shadow in the body— the disease —would go. The following story seeks to illustrate these points.

John asked to see me about the chronic pain at the base of his neck. He was somewhat sceptical about experiencing this type of healing as he came from a scientific background. The neck pain had been present for some months and his hospital had advised a long course of physiotherapy. I explained to John that there was a part of his mind which knew exactly what the cause of this problem was. To help him to access this, I told him I would take him through a relaxation procedure and try some ways which might help him to let go of his rational mind so he could open to his inner wisdom.

I asked John to lie down and made him comfortable with

cushions and a blanket. Using a progressive relaxation method, I asked him to tense and release all the muscles in his body. Whilst he was doing this, I kept my hands lightly on his head as I find this helps me to join with the client as well as aiding their relaxation. I asked John to say a prayer to indicate his willingness to receive the help that is always there and to ask for help in seeing what thoughts he needed to change in his mind which would bring about healing. In my previous conversation with him I had discovered he was open to working with prayer. I joined his silent prayer with one of my own. I asked that I might open myself to my own source of help and be used as a channel in this healing session.

We remained in silence for a few minutes whilst I continued to lay on hands. I then asked John how he was feeling and if there was anything happening for him. He told me that the face of his aunt had appeared to him and had spoken the following words: 'This pain in your neck is vengeance upon yourself for what you did.' John told me that this was not said in any accusing manner but as a simple statement of fact. However, the words made no sense to John and we decided to leave this intriguing message for the moment. Although John had stressed that he had a well-developed logical, rational and scientific mind, I felt he also possessed strong intuition. I felt drawn to try some imagery in the form of a guided journey, to help lead him to his own source of inner wisdom.

I began the journey by asking him to visualise himself walking down a country lane on a summer's day. To encourage him to experience all his senses, I asked him to feel the road underfoot, smell the flowers, hear the sounds of nature and observe the surroundings and the sky above him. In this manner he became more involved with his inner world which, in turn, loosened the hold of his rational mind. I continued to guide him on his journey in nature, sometimes stopping to enable him to study some object of interest.

The goal of this journey was to connect John with some symbolic form of his inner wisdom or higher self — what the Course calls the Holy Spirit. However, this guided journey was soon to come to an abrupt end. I had thought that I was leading him through a forest when he stated, with some irritation, that he had tried four times to enter this forest without success. Each time he tried, the trees would turn into a white mist and the forest would disappear.

One of the maxims I work with in healing is: 'Anything you resist, persists — anything you accept can heal.' I told John to accept this mist, ask for help and continue to walk through it. As he continued, a human cell appeared in the mist surrounded by violet light. His scientific training enabled him to recognise it as a human cell and, further, to know that it was cancerous. Suddenly, the memory of his dying mother returned to him accompanied by strong feelings of guilt and shame. He told me he had felt unable to cope with the situation at the time and had given the care of his mother to his aunt. This was the same aunt who had appeared at the start of the healing session.

John began to cry tears he had been unable to shed at the time of his mother's illness. He realised he had repressed all his guilt and shame around this issue and now needed to obtain forgiveness. I encouraged him to 'invite' his mother into this session and express to her all the things he needed to say. I told John to imagine that his mother was really here in the room and to speak out loud to her. When he had finished, I asked him to listen to anything his mother wanted to say to him and to speak out loud what she said. In this way John was given an opportunity to share his buried feelings with his mother and forgive himself for his past actions.

I then asked John if he felt complete with his experience and to return his awareness to the room we were in. He told me that the pain in his neck felt much better and he now understood the significance of his aunt's remarks at the start of the session. His mother had died of cancer of the base of the neck and John felt his repressed guilt and shame over the handling of his mother's illness was reflected in his own bodily pain occurring in the identical area.

About four days later, just before John was leaving the Findhorn Foundation, I asked him about his neck pain and he told me that the improvement had been maintained. We had both experienced a powerful example of how the guilt in our mind is reflected in our bodily condition and how the power of forgiveness can dissolve both.

The above story is the first of a number of case histories which illustrate how healing can occur through forgiveness. I have chosen stories which have successful outcomes so that I can demonstrate what can be achieved when client and healer join together. There have, of course, been many instances when little or no progress has been achieved in healing sessions. The resistance of our ego to the healing process and the subject of the healed healer versus the unhealed healer will be covered in later chapters.

I was beginning to understand more clearly that only the mind is in need of healing, not the body. If the mind could regain its peace through forgiveness, then healing would be achieved. In Chapter 5, I shall explain more fully what I mean by forgiveness. Even if physical symptoms still remain after forgiveness has occurred, healing has taken place if peace of mind is the outcome. Looking back to when I first started to practise healing by laying on of hands, I now wondered what was really happening. In the Course I was to read:

> *It is not their hands that heal. It is not their voice that speaks the word of God. They merely give what has been given them.*
>
> (M18; M-5.III.2:8-10)

and, as previously stated:

> *False healing can indeed remove a form of pain and sick-*
> *ness. But the cause remains, and will not lack effects.*
>
> (S16: S-3.II.1:4-5)

I now saw that the use of my hands was but a form which helped me to join with my client. To join with another is to undo the ego's thought of separation and allow the love of God to return to our awareness. It is this love that undoes the guilt in the client's mind and allows the healing to take place. My function as a healer was to drop all judgement and criticism of my client. This then makes room for God's healing love to be extended from my mind to the client's mind. In the presence of that love and light, the client would have an opportunity to change their mind and forgive the past. I shall expand upon the subject of healing others in Chapter 7.

My challenge in a healing session is to reach a peaceful, centred and non-judgemental space and to withdraw any investment I might have in the outcome. The power of this has occasionally been demonstrated to me by some unintentional healings which have occurred over the years.

On one occasion a friend of mine was suffering from painful knees. This condition had started a couple of days earlier whilst she was watching television. The programme had made her fearful and when she got up from her chair both knees were painful. She stopped me in the corridor and asked for a healing session. I intuitively felt I should see her right away. I turned to her, put my hand on her shoulder and said that we could have a healing session now if that was convenient. She looked at me and said, 'Don't bother — the pain has just gone in both knees!'

There had been no intention on my part to heal in that moment and I became curious as to what had happened. When I analysed this and other times when spontaneous healings had occurred, I remembered that I was in a peaceful, joyful and accepting space. When we can temporarily lay our ego aside, there is no barrier to the presence of God's love in our mind. God's healing love is now free to flow spontaneously into the mind of the other person, giving them the opportunity to change their mind about the guilt they are carrying. When we are in a joyful and accepting state of mind we give them a different message about themselves in contrast to what their ego is telling them. We demonstrate they are not the sinful and guilty person that they thought they were and thus allow them to change their mind about themselves. This shift of perception, the miracle, allows them to forgive themselves and let their guilt, with its physical symptoms, disappear.

'... sickness is of the mind, and has nothing to do with the body.'

(M17; M-5.II.3:2)

Everyone who has ever come to me for a healing has, and must have, a resistance to being healed. In some part of their mind is the decision to get sick in the first place. We believe we gain benefits from our disease and do not want to lose these benefits through being healed. Thus there is usually a strong ambivalence towards the healing session and the healer, although this may be unconscious. The pamphlet *Psychotherapy: Purpose, Process and Practice* makes this point very clear:

> *The therapist is seen as one who is attacking the patient's most cherished possession; his picture of himself. And since this picture has become the patient's security as he perceives it, the therapist cannot but be seen as a real source of danger to be attacked and even killed. The psychotherapist then, has a tremendous responsibility. He must meet attack without attack and therefore without defence. It is his task to*

*demonstrate that defences are not necessary and that
defencelessness is strength.*

(P9; P-2.IV.9:5-6. 10:1-3)

David was a participant in a two-week workshop I was
giving at the Findhorn Foundation. During the first week
he became aware of a hatred he carried towards himself.
He felt the hatred to be 'located' in his solar plexus and
that its origin lay in the sexual abuse he had experienced
from his uncle when he was ten years old. He only realised
in the workshop setting that following the period of
abuse, he had repressed feelings of guilt and blame for
what had happened. This new awareness caused him
much discomfort and he developed asthma and a chest
infection by the end of the first week of the workshop.
David felt ashamed of his memories, did not want to
explore this issue with anyone and considered leaving the
workshop. He visited the local doctor and was given a
course of antibiotics.

During the start of the second week of the workshop,
David asked me for a private healing session. After a
period of relaxation and laying on of hands, I decided I
would try to get him to explore and accept the hatred he
was experiencing in his solar plexus. The Course states:
'There is an advantage to bringing nightmares into awareness, but only to teach that they are not real, and that anything they contain is meaningless.' (T159; T-9.V.3:1) If
David could uncover his 'nightmares' of self-hatred and
guilt without judging them, he would then have an opportunity to change his mind about his seeming 'sins' of the
past. My own feeling of acceptance and non-judgement
of him, which I experienced as I gently guided him on this
journey, would also help this process.

To help him undo his state of repression — what the
Course calls 'denial' — I asked him to explore the sensation in his solar plexus. Previous experience had taught

me that important messages are locked up in our areas of pain. I asked him to describe how large the area of discomfort was, its shape and depth, its colour and texture, and whether it felt hotter or colder than the rest of his body. As it is impossible to resist and explore the pain simultaneously, I was encouraging David to undo his denial about himself. When clients follow this approach, they are describing the 'clothes of the messenger' and this can lead them into deeper levels of their mind where the 'nightmares' are to be found.

David discovered a hard red ball in his solar plexus. I asked this 'messenger' how it was feeling and David replied that it was angry. He experienced a strong resistance to his discovery. He could not accept it in his body and hated it being there. He said it felt like a foreign object which needed to be attacked and thrown out. Feeling his strong resentment towards this part of his body, I went within and asked for help in what to say or do. What came to me was to ask him how this hard, red, angry ball had served him all these years. After all, it was his creation and he was holding on to it with great determination. Not surprisingly, he objected strongly to my question and reiterated he did not want this ball inside him. I felt guided to continue gently exploring this issue with him without any investment on my part in trying to bring about changes in him that I thought were necessary.

Slowly David began to receive insights on how this ball of hatred was serving him. He realised that he had created it as a protection against his fear of opening his heart to people and acting more spontaneously in life. He saw himself as a person dominated by his mind and rigid control patterns. To let go of his investment in his self-hatred and guilt was to free himself to relate more lovingly and openly to people. This opportunity was now before him. He could hear two parts of his mind counselling him: the ego and the Holy Spirit. His ego told him that it would be very dangerous to let go of his control patterns, as he would not be able to predict how people would behave to him if he related more from his heart than his head. The Holy Spirit part of his mind counselled him in the opposite direction.

He had nothing to lose but an illusion of sacrifice. The new way of relating would bring him renewed energy and joy. David could also sense a suppressed part of himself he called the 'joker' and felt it would be fun to let this joker out. As he struggled with these two voices, I asked him if he would try and see if he could give away his angry red ball. I reassured him it would be okay if he could not, but he could lose nothing by the experiment. I suggested he visualise a pair of loving, gentle, golden hands outstretched before him awaiting the gift of his angry red ball. I told him that these hands wanted his pain, not his love, as a gift. The hands were only interested in 'removing the blocks to the awareness of love's presence' (Intro, Text) in him. David decided to give his pain away to these hands. As he did this, he started to laugh and cry at the same time. A lightness of being came over him and a strong energy entered his body, so much so that after the session he went off to run and literally jump in the nearby woods. Although he had been on the point of leaving the workshop, he now felt happy to stay and complete it.

The Course lists a number of reasons why we choose sickness and we shall explore these in Chapter 4. We are not usually aware of these decisions, as our ego immediately denies having made them. Thus it appears we are innocent victims of circumstances beyond our control. We say to ourselves that our body is sick and our body needs healing, forgetting that the causative level of disease is in our mind.

Everyone in this world seems to have his own special problems. Yet they are all the same, and must be recognised as one if the one solution that solves them all is to be accepted . . . The temptation to keep the problem as many is the temptation to keep the problem of separation (from God) unsolved . . . If you could recognise that your only problem is separation, no matter what form it takes, you would accept the answer because you would see its relevance.

from *A Course in Miracles*
(W139; W-pI.79.2:1-2, 4:1, 6:2)

Chapter Two

One Problem, One Solution

This chapter summarises some of the teachings of *A Course in Miracles* with regard to the nature of reality. These teachings are central to understanding that everything we experience comes from a mental origin. We live in a mental, not a physical, universe and everything is an idea. By changing our mind, we can change the way we perceive the world, our body, disease and suffering, and achieve a state of inner peace and joy.

The ideas presented here may seem quite strange and even shocking. However, it is important to grasp these principles in order to reach an understanding of the cause of disease. I experienced great difficulty when I first studied the metaphysics of the Course. In fact, I took the advice of my ego and denied that there were any metaphysics in the Course, even though I had read and re-read them for some six years!

It was not until Ken and Gloria Wapnick came to the Findhorn Foundation to give a workshop that I seriously looked at my fear around this issue. During that weekend Ken asked me who I thought created the physical universe. Like most people I carried a comforting image of a kind father God who had created the universe and was looking after it all including me. As I began to study this area of the Course an altogether different picture emerged. I came to see that the metaphysics in the Course were at the heart of its teachings and that it is a wonderful message of hope. It has given me a key to understand the cause of our suffering and where true healing must take place.

The Course teaches us that 'this world you seem to live in is not home to you'. (W331; W-pI.182.1:1) Our reality is not in this world of form which is made within the confines of space and time. Here we experience separation, limits, imperfection and death. What God created is like Himself — perfect, eternal, limitless, formless and changeless. This is who we really are and this can never be harmed by what we do. We are ideas in the Mind of God and were created perfect for all eternity:

> *Father, I was created in Your Mind, a holy Thought that never left its home. I am forever Your Effect, and You forever and forever are my Cause. As You created me I have remained. Where You established me I still abide. And all Your attributes abide in me, because it is Your Will to have a Son so like his Cause that Cause and Its Effect are indistinguishable.*
>
> (W454; W-pII.326.1:1-5)

Our true home is Heaven, and our true function is co-creation with God. Heaven is not a place but a state of perfect unity between God and his creation — the Christ or Son of God:

> *Heaven is not a place nor a condition. It is merely an awareness of perfect oneness, and the knowledge that there is nothing else.*
>
> (T359; T-18.VI.1:5-6)

Heaven cannot be described using language, for language pertains to the world of form. Heaven can only be experienced in this world through revelation which is a mystical experience. In our world we learn through our senses, whilst in Heaven there is no learning, for we were given everything at our creation. Learning implies time, and there is no time in Heaven.

You may be wondering, if the abstract perfection of Heaven is our true home, what then are we doing in this imperfect world of form? Although this is a good question, it does imply that we really are here and that separation from God is a fact. The Course states that we have fallen asleep in Heaven and are dreaming of this separated state.

You dwell not here, but in eternity.
You travel but in dreams, while safe at home.

(T240; T-13.VII.17:6-7)

You are at home in God, dreaming of exile but
perfectly capable of awaking to reality.

(T169; T-10.I.2:1)

Thus our whole lives are spent in dreams. When we wake up in the morning, we still continue to dream but in other forms. Our waking dream seems very real to us and the Course does not ask us to deny what we believe. However, through the practice of forgiveness we can begin to undo our belief in separation and start the process of waking up until, finally, we regain our awareness of Heaven.

The ego is a thought we have created in our mind. It is the idea that separation from God is possible to achieve.

Into eternity, where all is one, there crept a tiny, mad idea,
at which the Son of God remembered not to laugh.

(T544; T-27.VIII.6:2)

This idea that there could be something different from the perfect unity of Heaven, and that we could take the role of God away from Him, is impossible to achieve. However, it is possible to dream that we have achieved it and this is what we have done. Our universe has become the ego's playground where it can pretend that it is God. Our true function of co-creation with God has been replaced by the miscreation of our ego. This universe is not physical in nature but is an idea in the mind of the sleeping Son of God. And ideas can be changed!

The world you see is an illusion of a world. God did not cre-
ate it, for what He creates must be eternal as Himself. Yet

*there is nothing in the world you see that will endure for-
ever. Some things will last in time a little while longer than
others. But the time will come when all things visible will
have an end.*

(M8l; C-4.1:1-5)

Figure 2.1[4] is an aid to understanding this concept.

For reasons we cannot comprehend, part of the mind
of Christ fell asleep and dreamt that separation from his
Father had been achieved. The Son's mind is analogous
to a film projector onto which a film of separation has been
loaded. These thoughts become projected images 'out
there' in the world, which are now perceived as separate
objects. We believe we are on this screen moving around
in the physical universe. Not only do we now believe we
have achieved our desire to be a creator like God, we also
believe we have stolen God's power and taken his function. The universe now serves a dual function for us. As
well as 'proving' that we have succeeded in doing better
than God, it also acts as a place where God cannot enter
and thus saves us from his avenging anger.

*The body is a tiny fence around a little part of a glorious
and complete idea. It draws a circle, infinitely small, around
a very little segment of Heaven, splintered from the whole,
proclaiming that within it is your kingdom, where God can
enter not.*

(T364; T-18.VIII.2:5-6)

What I have described above is not in our conscious
awareness. We cannot tolerate the memory of what we
think we have done to God. In our arrogance, we think
we have smashed Heaven into thousands of pieces and
created a better alternative in its place. This insane belief
produces a deep sense of wrongdoing which the Course

4 Figures 2.1 and 2.2 are based on ideas found in *Awaken From the Dream*
by Gloria and Kenneth Wapnick. (See Recommended Books & Tapes.)
I recommend this book to those who would like to pursue these introductory ideas more deeply.

Projection Makes Perception
— The making of a world —

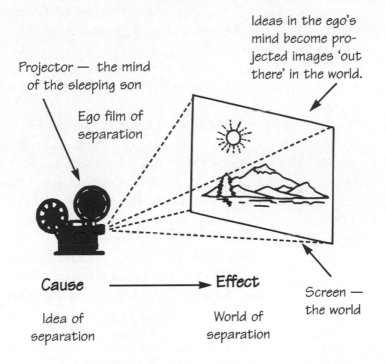

Projector — the mind
of the sleeping son

Ego film of
separation

Ideas in the ego's
mind become pro-
jected images 'out
there' in the world.

Cause ⟶ **Effect**

Idea of
separation

World of
separation

Screen —
the world

What I see reflects a process in my mind, which starts with my idea of what I want. From there, the mind makes up an image of the thing the mind desires, judges valuable, and therefore seeks to find. These images are then projected outward, looked upon, esteemed as real and guarded as one's own. From insane wishes comes an insane world. From judgement comes a world condemned.   W454; WpII.325.1:1-5

Fig 2.1

refers to as sin, and we have denied and pushed this deeply into our unconscious mind. But to deny something does not prevent it having power over us. This sense of sin produces guilt in us and a fear of justified punishment for our wrongdoing. The Course states that this is the origin of our feelings of inferiority, self-hate, lack of self-worth and bodily disease. Every problem we think we have, whether psychological or physical, can be traced to just one problem — the belief that we have separated from our Creator.

It would be impossible to wake up from this convincing dream without the presence of the Holy Spirit in our mind. As we fell asleep in Heaven, God placed the Holy Spirit in our mind as the correction for our dream. The Course calls this plan of correction 'the Atonement' and its goal is to undo our belief in the ego's thought of separation. The Holy Spirit is variously referred to in the Course as the Voice for God, Teacher, Comforter, Guide and Mediator. His shining presence in our mind can undo all our ego dreams of darkness if we but turn to Him for help. Because of the presence of the Holy Spirit in one part of our mind, we cannot completely forget our real home.

> *Listen — perhaps you catch a hint of an ancient state not quite forgotten; dim, perhaps, and yet not altogether unfamiliar, like a song whose name is long forgotten, and the circumstances in which you heard completely unremembered. Not the whole song has stayed with you, but just a little wisp of melody, attached not to a person or a place or anything particular. But you remember, from just this little part, how lovely was the song, how wonderful the setting where you heard it, and how you love those who were there and listened with you.*
>
> (T416; T-21.I.6:1-3)

When the thought of separation was taken seriously, the One-mindedness of Christ appeared to fragment into three parts — the ego, the Holy Spirit and the decision

Truth and Illusion

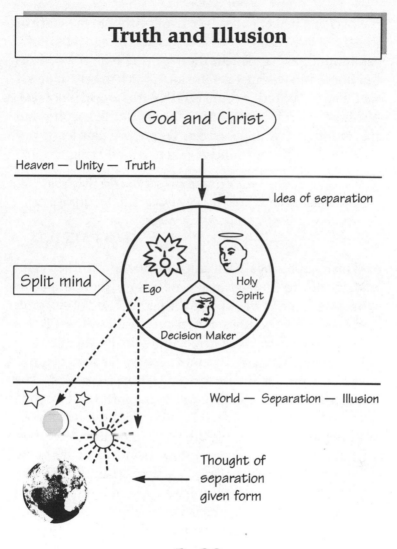

Fig 2.2

maker or sleeping Son of God. See Figure 2.2 which illustrates the separation from God and the splitting of our mind.

The term 'decision maker' originated from Kenneth Wapnick and although it is not used in the Course it is implied throughout the book. Every moment of our day, the decision maker chooses to listen either to the voice of the ego or the Voice of the Holy Spirit. The ego tells us the separation has happened, the world is real, the body is our home and we must defend and attack to get our needs met. The Holy Spirit's counsel is that this world is not real, our home is in Heaven, our reality is formless spirit and the world is but a classroom where we can learn our lessons of forgiveness and awaken from our nightmare.

> *The ego made the world as it perceives it, but the Holy Spirit,*
> *the reinterpreter of what the ego made, sees the world as a*
> *teaching device for bringing you home.*
>
> (T74; T-5.III.11:1)

This chapter has been an introduction to the metaphysics of the Course. It is a necessary foundation for what is to come as we explore the ego's world of sin, guilt and fear and the bodily sickness produced by these states of mind. As we slowly learn to allow the love of the Holy Spirit to undo the ego's thought system, we shall begin to awaken from our dream of separation from God. The peace of God will begin to return to our mind and we shall use our body as a vehicle for loving communication. As we lose our belief that we are sinful creatures, our body will automatically experience good health and vitality. We shall come to perceive it simply as an instrument of learning for the mind, with no intrinsic value in itself. When we have completed all our lessons of forgiveness, we shall be happy to lay our body aside.

> *O my brothers, if you only knew the peace that will envelop*
> *you and hold you safe and pure and lovely in the mind of*
> *God, you could but rush to meet Him where His altar is.*
> *Hallowed your name and His, for they are joined here in*
> *this holy place. Here he leans down to lift you up to Him,*
> *out of illusions into holiness; out of the world and to eter-*
> *nity; out of all fear and given back to love.*
>
> (M82; C-4.8:1-3)

Perception is a mirror, not a fact. And what I look on is my state of mind, reflected outward ... Everything you perceive is a witness to the thought system you want to be true ...What you project you disown, and therefore do not believe it is yours.

from *A Course in Miracles*
(W441; W-pII.304.1:3-4; T192;
T-II.V.18:3; T89; T-6.II.2:1)

Chapter Three

The Ego's World of Denial and Projection

In the writing of this chapter, as well as parts of Chapter 4, I have been greatly assisted by the scholarship of Kenneth Wapnick. In particular I have utilised some of the ideas and models he presented in *Forgiveness and Jesus* (see Recommended Books & Tapes) in explaining some of the concepts in these two chapters.

This morning you believe you woke up. The dreams of last night have faded and the 'reality' of a new day has begun. But has it? We saw in the previous chapter that any state outside Heaven is not real. The Course states this as follows:

> *There is no life outside of Heaven. Where God created life, there life must be. In any state apart from Heaven life is illusion.*
>
> (T459; T-23.II.19:1-3)

Figure 3.1 illustrates this, again using the analogy of a cinema.

The decision maker has chosen to listen to the ego instead of the Holy Spirit. The ego thought — that the separation is real — is believed by the decision maker and is projected out by the 'lens' of the mind as an image of the world. In this analogy, the screen is our world. When we fall asleep and dream, the events and people seem very real to us. We eat dream food, ride in dream cars and communicate with dream people. Our body may become sick and even die. People may seek to harm us and monsters can appear to frighten us. But when we wake up, our fears are gone for we realise it was all a dream.

The Dream World of the Ego

The ego's world of space and time

The split mind

All your time is spent in dreaming. Your sleeping and your waking dreams have different forms, and that is all. Their content is the same.   T351; T-18.II.5:12-14

Fig 3.1

When we wake up from our night time dreams, our desire to remain separate from God is still with us. Our allegiance to the ego's thought system remains unchanged and so we create for ourselves a second dream which is no more real than the first. In this 'waking dream' we continue to act as we did in our sleeping dream. We believe that circumstances 'out there' in the world affect us. Certain people and events cause us to be happy and healthy, whilst other people and events cause us to be unhappy and sick. We seem to be the effect of causes that originate in the world. From this idea comes the deep-rooted sense that we are victimised by events we cannot control.

Whilst we believe that the cause of our happiness or pain lies outside our mind in a real world, we shall never know the peace and joy that is the goal of the Course. This illusory world is so convincing that without the help of the Holy Spirit we would never wake up. If we allow Him to, the Holy Spirit will transform the purpose of this world from one of separation to that of a classroom in which we can learn forgiveness and awaken from the dream into the joyous reality of who we really are. Thus this world can be used for the opposite purpose to that for which it was originally meant, transforming it from a place of despair to one of hope and meaning.

> *My salvation comes from me . . . The seeming cost of accepting today's idea is this: It means that nothing outside yourself can save you; nothing outside yourself can give you peace. But it also means that nothing outside yourself can hurt you, or disturb your peace or upset you in any way.*
>
> (W118; W-pI.70.2:1-2)

The Course is telling us that nothing in the ego's illusory world has the power to affect us unless we decide that it can. It is obvious that most of us do believe we are victims of the world. We tell ourselves that if only circumstances were different, we would be happy. If only we had had a better education, or if our parents had been more loving, or if we had not been abused as a child, or if only the weather/government/food etc was better, then we would be happy. We believe that if we could change the world, we would find the happiness that has always eluded us.

*The ego's plan for salvation centres around holding griev-
ances. It maintains that, if someone else spoke or acted differently, if some external circumstance or event were
changed, you would be saved. Thus, the source of salvation
is constantly perceived as outside yourself. Each grievance
you hold is a declaration, and an assertion in which you
believe, that says, 'If this were different, I would be saved.'
The change of mind necessary for salvation is thus demanded of everyone and everything except yourself.*

(W120; W-pI.71.2)

Denial

If we are to retain our allegiance to the ego's thought system, we must never question where the real source of our
suffering lies — in our separated mind and not in the
world. Our ego's thoughts maintain a protective wall
against the love of the Holy Spirit. Our constant judgement of ourselves and others maintains this barrier to the
illuminating light of God. The diagram in Figure 3.2 came
to my wife Salice in meditation and illustrates the above
statement.

If we are to find peace, we must question the counsel
of the ego as to the origin of our physical and psychological suffering. We created the ego's thought system as a
direct challenge to God's creation. The ego was born out
of competition and hate and thus contains these traits
within itself. It too wishes to survive and, in turn, has no
love for its maker, the sleeping Son of God.

*You do not love what you made, and what you made does
not love you. Being made out of denial of the Father, the ego
has no allegiance to its maker.*

(T55; T-4.III.4:2-3)

In its desire to be autonomous and take the place of
God, the ego uses two powerful mechanisms of denial

'The Holy Spirit is the radiance that you must let banish the idea of darkness' T69; T5.II.4:2

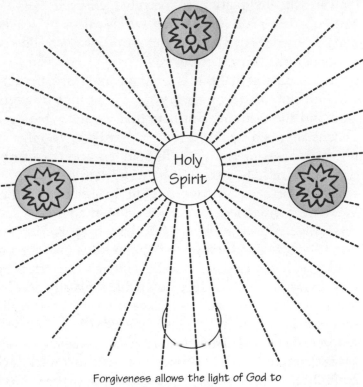

Holy Spirit

Forgiveness allows the light of God to dispel the darkness

The ego makes illusions. Truth undoes its evil dreams by shining them away. Truth never makes attack. It merely is. And by its presence is the mind recalled from fantasies, awaking to the real. Forgiveness bids this presence enter in, and take its rightful place within the mind. Without forgiveness is the mind in chains, believing in its own futility. Yet with forgiveness does the light shine through the dream of darkness, offering it hope, and giving it the means to realise the freedom that is its inheritance.

W458; W-pII.332.1

Fig 3.2

and projection to keep us believing in it. These ego defence mechanisms keep us, the decision maker, focused on the world. The illusion is so powerful that we easily feel justified in our victimhood. The Course cautions us to 'beware the temptation to perceive yourself unfairly treated'. (T523; T-26.X.4:1) When we fell asleep in Heaven and dreamed we had created this world, we also allowed a 'veil of forgetfulness' to be drawn over our decision. We denied to ourself that this is what we had done, because we could not stand the memory of our seeming sin against God and the resulting self-hate that we felt. This deep unconscious sin against God manifests as feelings of unworthiness, inferiority (or its compensation of superiority), lack of self-worth, self-hate and self-loathing.

The Course uses the word 'guilt' to describe all this. We never seem to feel good enough, no matter how successful we appear in the eyes of the world. We feel we don't deserve good things to happen to us and need to work very hard before we can allow ourselves a little pleasure. In fact, we believe deep down that we really deserve to be punished for what we have done to God. 'Guilt deserves punishment' is a psychological law. This was graphically shown to me during a period of my life when I was listening to the teachings of J. Krishnamurti. Incidentally, his teachings have many parallels to the Course, especially in the area of thought. He teaches that it is our ego thinking which blocks the awareness of who we really are.

I had been attending Krishnamurti's talks in England and Switzerland for twelve years but I had never spoken to him. It was very difficult to get an interview with him and I had never thought even to try. One time, after listening to one of his talks, I went to the meal tent and helped myself to some food. I was walking inside the tent when I suddenly found myself a couple of feet away from Krishnamurti. He was quietly sitting on a chair eating his food. I had not been thinking of him at that moment and was taken by surprise. He looked at me intently and maintained his somewhat serious expression. As I looked at him, I spontaneously felt love and appreciation welling up within me for this man but I did not move or say anything to him. His face suddenly changed and broke into a beautiful smile. His eyes filled with love, he put his plate down, stood up, opened his arms and moved towards me. Here was the realisation of my dream. I was about to meet the man I most admired in the world. And what did I do? I turned and walked quickly away! I could not take that love. I felt I did not deserve it and would be overwhelmed by it.

When I reached the end of the tent I took a furtive look back. He was talking with another person and I knew it would be pointless to try and speak to him again. Now I pray to experience the love of Jesus, but am I ready for that? Obviously not or I would have accepted it. We always have what we want to have, which is mostly sin, guilt and fear. I still prefer my ego to Jesus but I am also aware that the days of my allegiance to the ego are numbered. I will go home, as will everyone else, but the time it takes is up to each of us to decide.

> *Tolerance for pain may be high, but it is not without limit. Eventually everyone begins to recognise, however dimly, that there must be a better way. As this recognition becomes more firmly established, it becomes a turning point.*
>
> (T18: T-2.III.3:5-7)

When we separated from God, if we had turned to the guidance of the Holy Spirit in our split mind, He would have told us to 'laugh gently' at the ego's insane thoughts of separation and autonomy. But already our allegiance and belief in the ego was too strong. The ego's counsel made us afraid of the Holy Spirit, for was He not of God and look what we had done to God's Kingdom. We had destroyed the unity of Heaven, stolen God's creative power and left. In our madness we now believed God was angry with us and demanded vengeance and sacrifice from us.

This is the origin of all the passages in the Bible which depict an avenging and angry father who is out for our blood. No wonder we became afraid of the Holy Spirit in our mind. He was God's agent and not to be trusted. In our terror we could only turn to the ego and ask for its help in our fear of God's justified punishment. The ego's reply, as it always is, was to deny and project our guilt onto a non-existent world. The ego has created an illusory problem (separation from God) and now proceeds to counsel us endlessly on how to solve it through denial and projection. Our ceaseless busyness and giving importance to the details of the ego's world of form, makes an excellent smokescreen to the presence of the Holy Spirit in our mind, thus ensuring the survival of the ego. Our very first act was to deny that we had ever had this 'battle' with God in the first place. The Course describes this first denial as follows:

> *Forget the battle. Accept it as a fact, and then forget it. Do not remember the impossible odds against you. Do not remember the immensity of the 'enemy', and do not think about your frailty in comparison. Accept your separation, but do not remember how it came about. Believe that you have won it, but do not retain the slightest memory of Who your great 'opponent' really is.*

(M43; M-17.6:5-10)

This denial is so effective that we believe we have nothing to do with this world which we are born into. We are not responsible for what we find here and feel justified in blaming God when His creation does not work so well. But as we have seen, this world is not God's creation but the miscreation of the ego, which carries its own thought system into every detail of our world. As the ego's thought system is based on differences, comparison, separation, judgement, attack, defence, murder etc, so must it be reflected in the world, for as the Course states: 'Ideas leave not their source, and their effects but seem to be apart from them.' (T515; T-26.VII.4:7)

Every living thing on this planet must murder in order to live. We must kill vegetables or animals to survive. The animal kingdom must constantly spend its time either killing some other life form or protecting itself from being killed. Kill or be killed is at the heart of the ego's thought system, the ego believing it has killed God and stolen His power. This thought system must in turn become projected out as the image of the ego's world. This world is literally the image of the thoughts in the ego's mind. It cannot be anything else. If it is on the film, it must be on the screen. Therefore it is pointless to change what is on the screen; we must change what is on the film. The Course asks us to '. . . seek not to change the world, but choose to change your mind about the world'. (T415: T-21.Intro.1:7)

We need to remove the film of separation and attack, and replace it with the Holy Spirit's film of joining and forgiveness. Then the world will appear completely different to us, even though its form is still the same. Now we shall see through the eyes of the Holy Spirit and see people either 'asking for love or extending love' and nothing else. This is the judgement of the Holy Spirit which Jesus manifested into this world. Knowing who he really was, an immortal, formless child of God, Jesus had no need of defence, and knowing we were the same as him, he had no need to attack. Most of us are far from this realisation, however, and the Course warns us not to deny our bodies and our experience in this world.

Conflict must be resolved. It cannot be evaded, set aside, denied, disguised, seen somewhere else, called by another

name, or hidden by deceit of any kind, if it would be escaped.
It must be seen exactly as it is, where it is thought to be, in
the reality which has been given it, and with the purpose
that the mind accorded it. For only then are its defences
lifted, and the truth can shine upon it as it disappears.

(W459; W-pII.333.1:1-4)

Projection

In our daily lives, our hidden guilt is constantly being
triggered. For example, someone pushes into the queue
in front of us, a car forces us to slow down by suddenly
cutting in front of us, a person insults us. We usually experience 'justified anger' in these circumstances, not realising that the source of our pain is really in our mind and
nothing to do with these events in the world. Our ego
would automatically advise us to attack back, either
expressing our anger at the people involved or projecting
our anger internally, eventually resulting in sickness in
the body, e.g. a headache, stomach ulcer, asthma attack.
To the ego either is satisfactory for it focuses our attention
onto the world (where the problem is not) and away from
our mind (where the cause is). See Figure 3.3.

While I was living at the Findhorn Foundation, a
woman who had been ill for three weeks approached me
for a healing session. She had flu-like symptoms and a
persistent cough which kept her awake at night. During
the relaxation stage of the healing session, as I was holding my hands above her chest, she began to feel an uncom-
fortable sensation in that area. I wanted her to explore this
as I felt it contained some insight for her. To help her accept
the discomfort, I asked her to describe what she felt or
saw in her chest. She said that it felt as if there was a closed
wooden gate there. I asked her what she wanted to do
with that gate, thinking she might gently open it. Instead,
in her mind's eye, she took a large hammer and smashed

Guilt Must Be Projected

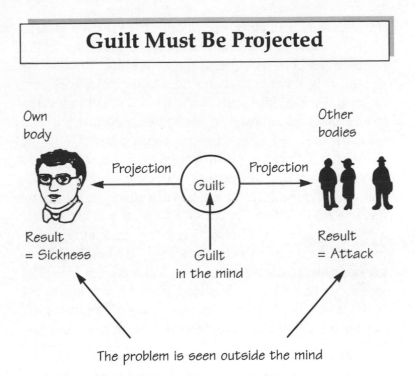

Own body

Other bodies

Projection ← Guilt → Projection

Result = Sickness

Guilt in the mind

Result = Attack

The problem is seen outside the mind

Fig 3.3

the gate to pieces. Suddenly she became aware of an intense anger that was focused in this area of her body. As she became aware of it, it moved higher up and lodged in her throat. This caused a coughing fit to occur.

Pursuing the approach of helping her to accept what was there, I asked her to describe how her throat appeared to her. She first described it as a hard red ball but it suddenly changed into a picture of a tall, black, ugly looking monster. She was very disturbed at seeing this image in her mind. I knew the picture of the monster was an important messenger carrying information about what was denied in her unconscious. It was important for her to accept this new picture and not to resist it. I encouraged her to try and make friends with the image but she found this very difficult. However, at one point she felt guided to give it a gift. She saw herself take a golden chain out of her heart and clasp it around the neck of the monster. As she did this, its eyes changed from being cold, hard and angry to eyes of love and compassion. I encouraged her to approach the monster to see if she could touch it. She was able to stroke it for a few moments only.

At that point, the healing session finished. She had become aware that during these three weeks of illness she had been denying strong feelings of anger. The following day she told me that her cough had disappeared shortly after the session had finished and the remaining symptoms of her illness had also now gone. We had both been given a powerful example of the effect of denial. Her original anger had been internalised, creating sickness in the body. It was here that she thought the problem lay until she undid her denial, accepted the pain in her mind and let it go.

Sickness is anger taken out on the body, so that it will suffer pain.

(T560: T-28.VI.5:1)

The ego's constant plan is to reverse cause and effect and keep us from looking at the cause of our distress which is in our mind, for if we were to return to our mind, we could also discover the presence of the Holy Spirit and listen to Him instead of the ego. This is the last thing the ego wants, for that would lead to its own death. Its constant chant to us is that the problem is in the world and not the mind and such is the power of this illusion that we choose to believe its advice. As we seek to blame the world for our distress, by denying and projecting our problems, our guilt will only increase, for on some level we know denial and projection is not justified and we must eventually take responsibility for the separation ourselves.

Wrong-Mindedness
The ego's thought system

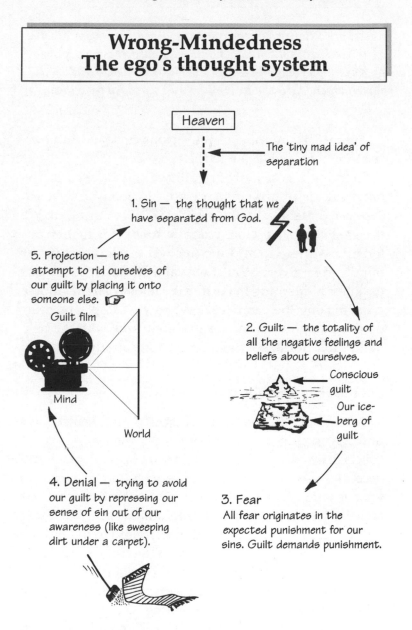

Heaven

The 'tiny mad idea' of separation

1. Sin — the thought that we have separated from God.

5. Projection — the attempt to rid ourselves of our guilt by placing it onto someone else. ☞

Guilt film

Mind

World

2. Guilt — the totality of all the negative feelings and beliefs about ourselves.

Conscious guilt

Our ice-berg of guilt

4. Denial — trying to avoid our guilt by repressing our sense of sin out of our awareness (like sweeping dirt under a carpet).

3. Fear
All fear originates in the expected punishment for our sins. Guilt demands punishment.

Fig 3.4

Yet projection will always hurt you. It reinforces your belief in your own split mind, and its only purpose is to keep the separation going. It is solely a device of the ego to make you feel different from your brothers and separated from them.

(T89: T-6.II.3:1-2)

Figure 3.4[5] summarises the vicious circle we find ourselves in when we listen to the ego.

In trying to get rid of our guilt, we only increase it. The only way out of this circular trap is to open ourselves to the ever-present help of the Holy Spirit in our mind. We need a shift of perception, a miracle, to see the situation differently. We need to find and uncover the darkness in our mind and forgive it. Whilst we value denial, we keep our darkness hidden and make it real. This is what the Course calls 'making the error real'. When we accept our murderous thoughts we can forgive them and, with the help of the Holy Spirit, see them for the illusions that they are.

Special Hate Relationships

Selecting special people to project our unhealed and unforgiven guilt onto is referred to in the Course as the special hate relationship. Any time we lose our peace and become upset over someone, we have met a mirror to what is unforgiven in ourselves. Our ego tells us that our anger is justified and we should attack back. The Holy Spirit counsels us to look within our mind to the hidden darkness and bring it to the light of the Holy Spirit so He can shine it away. The Holy Spirit constantly asks us to undo our denial, bring our projections back to our own mind and ask Him for help in letting them go.

If greedy people upset us, there is greed in our own mind. If angry people upset us, then anger is in our own

5 Figs 3.4 and 3.5 are based on ideas found in *Forgiveness and Jesus* by Kenneth Wapnick. (See Recommended Books & Tapes)

mind. Often the form is different, but the content never is. Perhaps you have never shown anger but are still judgemental when others get angry. However, if you look more closely at your mind, you will find the anger even though it might be tightly controlled and denied. You may say that people who smoke upset you and you have never smoked. But what does smoking represent to you? Perhaps you feel that smokers are insensitive, selfish and indifferent. If you look honestly within yourself, you will also find these traits even though you express them in a different form. This is why the Course says:

> *All anger is nothing more than an attempt to make some-one feel guilty, and this attempt is the only basis the ego accepts for special relationships . . . Anger is never justi-fied. Attack has no foundation.*
>
> (T297; T-15.VII.10:3; T593; T-30.VI.1:1-2)

It is important to note that the Course is not con-demning anger and saying we should not indulge our-selves in it. It simply states that it is not justified. In using anger we hope that our enemy will become guilty and admit to being the cause of our distress. He is now the one with the problem and not us.

We all have a tremendous investment in anger because we hold the magical belief that it will get us what we want. However, all it ever gets us is more guilt, for on some level we know our attack is unjustified. We are only attacking in another what we have in ourselves. To get rid of this increase in guilt our ego counsels us to get angry again. The ego's vicious circle of guilt and attack is thus main-tained and our allegiance to the ego is kept alive. This is not to say that we should suppress our anger for this only makes our guilt real. The Holy Spirit asks us to accept our anger and bring it to Him so He may release us from its illusion. This is difficult for most of us to do for we believe the object of our anger deserves our justified punishment and our anger gives us the energy to carry this out. It seems that if we let go of our anger the 'enemy' will get away without retribution.

Often people cite the Gospels in defence of their anger, for did not Jesus get angry in the temple and turn over the tables of the moneylenders? However, the Gospels did not say that Jesus got angry. Perhaps Jesus chose to teach in bold strokes that day. More importantly, Jesus taught directly against anger in his famous Sermon on the Mount.

Our defence of anger is understandable once we realise we believe that the source of our problems is in the world and we are innocent victims of circumstance. Once we drop our investment in anger, we will also lose our perception of ourselves as victims and turn to the Holy Spirit, and not the ego, for guidance. The ego sees this as a full frontal attack upon itself and will try everything to make us angry again. As we return to God, step by step, we must expect these attacks and pray for help. Anger is a major weapon of the ego, for it conceals the real source of the problem in our mind and makes us focus on the world instead. An experience which my wife Salice had around the time of the Gulf War in February 1992 illustrates our belief that our problems are in the world and not within us.

Salice was meditating and reflecting on Saddam Hussein and on the situation in Iraq and Kuwait, wanting to do something to help it. She felt helpless however and asked, 'What on earth can I do to help?' A voice in her mind said, 'How do you see Saddam Hussein?' Salice thought about this and immediately felt he was cruel, controlling, attacking and angry. The voice then asked, 'Do you have any of these traits?' Salice thought deeply and admitted that she did indeed manifest these traits at times. The voice then said, 'Fix these things in yourself and that is the greatest gift you can give the Gulf War.' She was then shown a picture of Saddam Hussein standing on top of a mountain with all the people of the world gathered around its base. Saddam Hussein was holding a large mirror and the light was glinting on it. He was saying, 'Look at me. You can't see these qualities inside yourselves so I am being a mirror for you and I have to exaggerate them in order for you to see them.' Salice said she knew in that moment that whilst she or anyone else has any negative quality, it is always eventually projected onto something or someone else.

Special Love Relationships

The special love relationship is the ego's chief weapon for keeping you from Heaven . . . (it) is but a shabby substitute for what makes you whole in truth, not in illusion.

(T317; T-16.V.2:3; T315; T-16.IV.8:4)

During our lifetime, we generally spend large amounts of time in dependent, needy relationships. These may be with our parents, friends, lovers, children, employers or anyone else we think will fulfil our needs. We also create dependence on food, money, alcohol, cigarettes, books, cars, clothes and other material items. All this is based on the idea that happiness must lie outside ourself in the ego's world of form. The Course refers to these forms as idols that are made to take the place of God's love for us (see quotation in Figure 3.5).

What is it that forces us to look outside ourself for peace and joy? When we broke our conscious link with our home in Heaven, we were left with a terrible emptiness inside our mind. The Course refers to this as 'the scarcity principle'. We felt there was something very important missing in our life but we were not consciously aware of what it was. The ego's mechanism of denial enabled us to hide our guilt but it also removed the memory of home. But we could not completely forget God and His Kingdom, so a faint, haunting memory remains.

This world you seem to live in is not home to you. And some-where in your mind you know that this is true. A memory of home keeps haunting you, as if there were a place that called you to return, although you do not recognise the voice, nor what it is the voice reminds you of. Yet still you feel an alien here, from somewhere all unknown.

(W331; W-pI.182.1:1-4)

Turning to the ego for its advice, it tells us that there is certainly something missing in us and the only solution to our misery is to look outside our mind and find it in the world. Once again, the ego's solution directs our search away from the love of the Holy Spirit in our mind and to the world outside and thus ensures the continuity of the ego. We now embark on a fruitless search for happiness where it cannot be found.

You must have noticed an outstanding characteristic of every end the ego has accepted as its own. When you have achieved it, it has not satisfied you.

(T144; T-8.VIII.2:5-6)

Our spiritual poverty may be translated into a search for money. However, we never seem to get enough to satisfy us. When we buy some new clothing, we often experience an initial satisfaction but then, some time later, we see another item which is more attractive than the one we bought previously and now we want this one. Or we may translate our need to rejoin with God as a need to join sexually with another body. We feel that frequent sexual union will be a satisfactory substitute for spiritual union. None of what has been written above is implying that the ego's world of form is sinful and should be avoided. This would make the 'error real' and lead to asceticism and self-debasement. Focusing on our unworthiness or escaping through pleasure-seeking serves the ego's goal of keeping us guilty and centred on the world. To the Holy Spirit, the world is but a classroom of experience where, instead of finding guilt, we may learn forgiveness and begin to awaken from the dream of separation. We need to be 'in the world but not of it', the middle path which the Buddha taught 2,500 years ago.

There is nothing like a relationship, irrespective of its form, to bring into our consciousness all that needs healing and forgiving in our mind. Without the mirror of relationship, our guilt would be difficult to discover. All our relationships must begin with the goal of fulfilling our ego needs. To direct unconditional love at one person is a contradiction in terms. When we finally awaken to who we really are, our love will extend to everyone equally and without exception. We thus need the relationships of this world to learn forgiveness.

Let us look more closely at what happens in a special love relationship. We will take as our example a co-dependent relationship between two lovers. However, what we are about to explore will apply to all forms of relationship which are based on needs. Feeling the pain and emptiness within us, we look for someone to fill this void. It is as if we had a bottomless pit inside our heart which we hope we can fill with something outside ourself. We look for a special someone with special characteristics. Our ego is always very selective and will make up an appropriate shopping list for us. On this list will be included what sort of body and characteristics we require in our partner — their age, shape, colour and degree of beauty, and whether they have a sense of humour or are kind, sensitive and caring.

The special relationship is totally meaningless without a body. If you value it, you must also value the body. And what you value you will keep. A special relationship is a device for limiting yourself to a body, and for limiting your perception of others to theirs.

(T321; T-16.VI.4 :1-4)

Perhaps we are looking for a 'protective father' or a 'kind mother' to look after us. Maybe instead we want a 'dependent child' so we feel needed and have someone to rescue. When we find someone who meets our needs (fulfils our shopping list) and we also meet their needs, a special love relationship is formed. The initial phase is often referred to as the honeymoon period, as both partners now experience happiness, feeling that at last their bottomless pits have been filled. They say they have fallen in love but the reality of the situation is that they have fallen into needs. Whilst the needs are mutually met, the partners are unaware that this relationship is but another special hate relationship with an attractive border surrounding it. Our partner continuously reminds us of our lack of self-worth, for the very reason that we are using them to fill our bottomless pit. We hate this lack of self-worth and guilt within us and so must hate those who remind us of it. Our dependence on our partner will breed contempt as we hate to rely on others. Thus the special relationship ends up increasing our pain and emptiness instead of reducing it as we had first unconsciously hoped. Here we see clearly the goal of all special relationships, both of hate and love, which is to create guilt and thus maintain our belief in the ego.

> Yet the closer you look at the special relationship, the more apparent it becomes that it must foster guilt and therefore must imprison.

> (T321; T-16.VI.3:4)

The ego has told us we are sinners and our guilt is the proof that the ego must be right. When our needs are no longer met, the buried hate for our partner comes to the surface and the ego tells us to project this onto them. Once again, our anger feels justified as we attempt to get our needs met by making our partner feel guilty. 'You told me you loved me but look how you treat me!' is a common ego ploy. Even if the relationship is repaired and we 'make up', a seed of doubt is sown at this point. This will increase each time a falling out occurs and doubt about the future of the relationship is registered. At this point, the ego may counsel us to find another more appropriate partner. This cycle can repeat itself over and over again where we continuously draw another partner and the same pattern re-emerges.

But we also have available to us the Holy Spirit's guidance, if we so desire it. If we turn to Him at any point in this cycle, He will tell us to change the goal of our relationship from special to holy so that we may learn His lessons of forgiveness. In Chapter 5 we shall explore the concept of the holy relationship in more detail. Figure 3.5 summarises the ego's vicious circle of the special love relationship.

Summary

Believing that the separation from God has really occurred we are left with a deep sense of sin and its attendant feeling of guilt. As previously stated, it is a psychological law that guilt demands punishment and we now fear this will happen to us. We turn to the ego to help us with this burden. Although the presence of the Holy Spirit would tell us we have nothing to fear — all is but a silly dream — we fear the Holy Spirit as He is an agent of an angry and vengeful God. The ego's counsel is simple — we need only deny that the separation from God ever happened as well as all the guilt we carry, and project it onto our relationships and the world in general. We are no longer the one with the problem, everyone and everything else is. What we hate about ourself we now deny and project onto our enemies (special hate relationships). Our anger towards them demands that they change their behaviour to restore our lost peace. Our problem is now seen outside ourself and is thus impossible to heal.

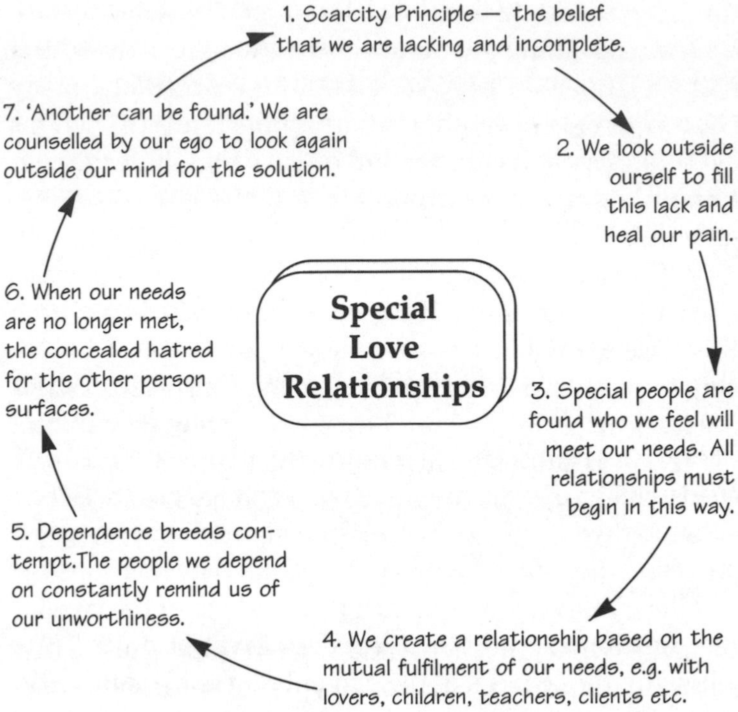

1. Scarcity Principle — the belief that we are lacking and incomplete.

7. 'Another can be found.' We are counselled by our ego to look again outside our mind for the solution.

2. We look outside ourself to fill this lack and heal our pain.

6. When our needs are no longer met, the concealed hatred for the other person surfaces.

Special Love Relationships

3. Special people are found who we feel will meet our needs. All relationships must begin in this way.

5. Dependence breeds contempt. The people we depend on constantly remind us of our unworthiness.

4. We create a relationship based on the mutual fulfilment of our needs, e.g. with lovers, children, teachers, clients etc.

No one who comes here but must still have hope, some lingering illusion, or some dream that there is something outside of himself that will bring happiness and peace to him. If everything is in him this cannot be so . . . . Seek not outside yourself. For it will fail, and you will weep each time an idol falls. Heaven cannot be found where it is not, and there can be no peace excepting there . . . . For all your pain comes simply from a futile search for what you want, insisting where it must be found. What if it's not there? Do you prefer that you be right or happy?   T573; T-29.VII.2:1-2, 1:1-9

Fig 3.5

The most powerful weapon the ego has against God is the special love relationship. Feeling there is something seriously lacking in us (called the scarcity principle) we look for special people (lovers, friends, parents, therapists etc) to fill our hole of despair with their attributes (money, admiration, sex, security, help and so on). Thus we seek a substitute for the only relationship that will satisfy us, our relationship with God, which we think we have lost forever.

The Holy Spirit would counsel us to use these very relationships as classrooms to learn forgiveness. The Holy Spirit can use everything the ego uses, but for the opposite purpose, i.e. to join instead of to separate. In our special love relationships we manipulate people to fulfil our needs, creating bargains where we exchange gifts between us which we think we need from each other. However, the unjustified attack within the special hate relationship and the manipulation and disguised attack of the special love relationship only increases our level of guilt. Thus following the counsel of the ego only increases our guilt, which is exactly what the ego always wanted, for now we will continue our faith in its reality. We created the ego thought system and it fights to survive. Its counsel maintains our sense of separation and keeps us in a vicious circle of guilt and attack.

All sickness comes from separation. When the separation is denied, it goes.

(T514; T-26.VII.2:1)

Figure 3.6 (overleaf) summarises our only choice — to listen to our ego and project, or to take the advice of the Holy Spirit and choose a miracle instead.

Projection or the Miracle
Our choice in the way we view the world

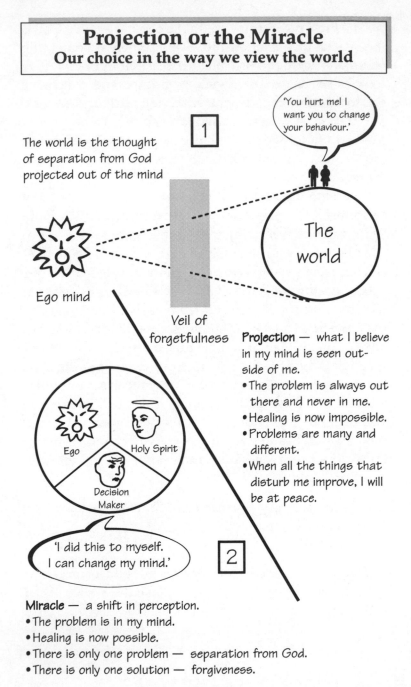

The world is the thought of separation from God projected out of the mind

1

'You hurt me! I want you to change your behaviour.'

The world

Ego mind

Veil of forgetfulness

Ego   Holy Spirit

Decision Maker

'I did this to myself. I can change my mind.'

2

Projection — what I believe in my mind is seen out-side of me.
- The problem is always out there and never in me.
- Healing is now impossible.
- Problems are many and different.
- When all the things that disturb me improve, I will be at peace.

Miracle — a shift in perception.
- The problem is in my mind.
- Healing is now possible.
- There is only one problem — separation from God.
- There is only one solution — forgiveness.

Fig 3.6

The body was not made by love. Yet love does not condemn it and can use it lovingly, respecting what the Son of God has made and using it to save him from illusions.

from *A Course in Miracles*
(T359: T-18.VI.4:7-8)

Chapter Four

Causes of Disease

The Role of the Body

The emphasis of the Course is not to heal the body but to achieve a joyful and peaceful mind. Once that has been accomplished, a healthy body will follow as a natural consequence. However, it is possible that someone could choose to have a disease so that a particular lesson can be learned more quickly. For example, a woman may decide that in order for her, and perhaps those around her, to learn more about faith and trust in God she will create a disease that will give her the opportunity to look within and discover an inner strength she intuitively knows she has, but has yet to experience. This decision to be ill will be made on a level of her mind of which she is not normally aware. There are many stories of people who have developed cancer and achieved spiritual breakthroughs in the process of working with their disease and its consequences on those around them. Such a person may still die of the cancer but the peace of mind obtained means that the mind has been healed. Thus we should not fall into the trap of judging others by the form of their illness, for we can never know all the facts.

The rest of this discussion on the cause of disease will focus on disease that is created by guilt in our mind. To heal our body, we need a miracle — a shift in perception — for disease is only a shadow on our body of the guilt in our mind. Jesus is well aware that this is not an easy task and that a compromise approach is often needed. As the Course says:

> Sometimes the illness has a sufficiently strong hold over the
> mind to render a person temporarily inaccessible to the

Atonement (correction of our errors). In this case, it may be wise to utilise a compromise approach to mind and body, in which something from outside (e.g. a pill) is temporarily given healing belief. This is because the last thing that can help the non-right-minded or the sick, is an increase in fear.

(T20; T-2.IV.4:5-7)

Thus there is nothing wrong in taking pills, remedies, having surgery or going to therapy. For real healing to occur, however, we must deal with the cause in our mind and not the effect on our body. To investigate the causes of disease, let us begin with the role of the body. See Figure 4.1.[6]

Kenneth Wapnick likens the mind, which is outside time and space, to a puppeteer, with the body and brain as a puppet. I think this is a good analogy to show the relationship between the two. A puppet can do nothing unless its strings are pulled by the puppeteer, who is normally hidden from view.

This gives the illusion that the puppet is self-motivated. In the same way, we are easily fooled by appearances that our body gets sick or well by itself. The whole focus of modern western medicine is to do something to the body. Of course, as long as we believe in the body and its 'laws' of operation, medicine will have an effect on the symptoms but it will not heal us. If the cause in the mind is not treated, the sickness will return in the same or a related form.

The body's health is fully guaranteed, because it is not limited by time, by weather or fatigue, by food and drink, or any laws you made it serve before.

(W252f; W-pI.136.18:3)

---

[6] The boxed quotation in Fig 4.1 is taken from the preface to the Course. The Arkana publication of the Course does not contain this preface.

'My Body is a Wholly Neutral Thing'
(Title of Lesson 294)

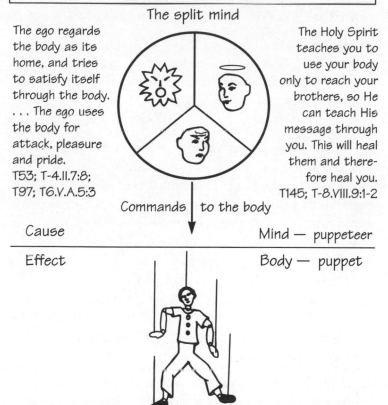

The split mind

The ego regards the body as its home, and tries to satisfy itself through the body. . . . The ego uses the body for attack, pleasure and pride.
T53; T-4.II.7:8; T97; T6.V.A.5:3

The Holy Spirit teaches you to use your body only to reach your brothers, so He can teach His message through you. This will heal them and therefore heal you.
T145; T-8.VIII.9:1-2

Commands to the body

Cause

Effect

Mind — puppeteer

Body — puppet

The body appears to be largely self-motivated and independent, yet it actually responds only to the intentions of the mind. If the mind wants to use it for attack in any form, it becomes prey to sickness, age and decay. If the mind accepts the Holy Spirit's purpose for it instead, it becomes a useful way of communicating with others, invulnerable as long as it is needed, and to be gently laid by when its use is over. Of itself it is neutral, as is everything in the world of perception. Whether it is used for the goals of the ego or the Holy Spirit depends entirely on what the mind wants.

Preface, 'What It Says'

Fig 4.1

The body, like every form in the universe, is a creation of the ego's thought system. However, we still have a choice in how we use it. In itself, it is neutral and can serve either the ego or the Holy Spirit's purpose.

My body, Father, cannot be Your Son. And what is not created cannot be sinful nor sinless; neither good nor bad. Let me, then, use this dream to help Your plan that we awaken from all dreams we made.

(W435; W-pII.294.2:1-3)

Whilst we allow the body to be the home of the ego, it will use it for its purpose of maintaining separation by judging and attacking. This attack will also manifest in the body as sickness. This serves the ego's purpose of concentrating our awareness on the body, which results in making the world appear very real and the Holy Spirit a liar. For we will say to ourself, 'Don't tell me this body isn't real — I'm in pain!' See Figure 4.2.

If, however, we allow the Holy Spirit to use the body as a tool of loving communication to enable Him to extend His message of forgiveness and joining, we will experience health as a result. As the Course states:

The Holy Spirit sees the body only as a means of communication and because communication is sharing, it becomes communion.

(T97; T-6.V.A.5:5)

When we experience pain in our body, it is tempting to pray to have it removed. The Course counsels us against this and instead asks us to pray to learn to forgive, because it is from unforgiveness that all our psychological and physical pain arises. When the hate, attack and anger in our mind is healed, its reflection in the body will disappear.

Pain is a wrong perspective. When it is experienced in any form, it is a proof of self-deception. It is not a fact at all. There is no form it takes that will not disappear if seen aright.

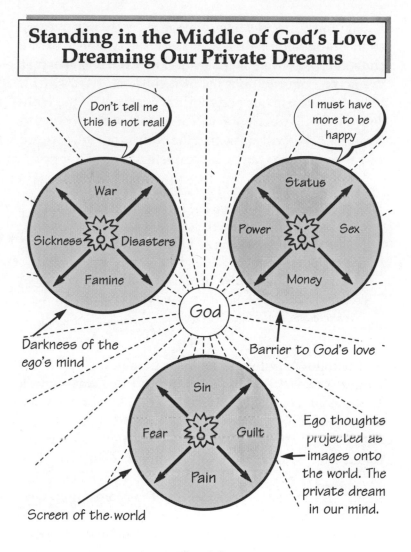

Fig 4.2

For pain proclaims God cruel . . . Pain is a sign illusions reign in place of truth. It demonstrates God is denied, confused with fear, perceived as mad, and seen as traitor to Himself. If God is real, there is no pain. If pain is real, there is no God.

(W351; W-pI.190.1:1-4, 3:1-4)

Our mind decides everything, even though we are often not aware of this. It chooses the moment of the body's birth as well as its death. The Course states that '. . . no one dies without his own consent'. (W274;W-pI. 152.1:4) If we use our body for the purposes of the Holy Spirit, we will experience no fear when the time comes to lay it aside. We will know that the body is not who we are and as our lessons are now complete, we can let it go.

> *When your body and your ego and your dreams are gone, you will know that you will last forever. Perhaps you think this is accomplished through death, but nothing is accomplished through death, because death is nothing. Everything is accomplished through life, and life is of the mind and in the mind. The body neither lives nor dies, because it cannot contain you who are life. If we share the same mind, you can overcome death because I did.*
>
> (T96; T-6.V.A.1:1-5)

The following story is an illustration of the power the mind has over the body. One evening, there was a knock on the door. I opened it to find a nervous young woman called Jane who had arranged to have a healing session with me that evening. Standing next to her was her girl-friend with whom she was in relationship and who had come to give her support. Jane was so nervous that her friend almost had to push her into the room. Upon talking with her it was apparent that she was afraid to be alone with a man. Her problem was that they both wanted a child and Jane was to be the mother. She had been trying artificial insemination for some time but with no success. Jane herself was a doctor and a medical colleague had informed her that she had a 'hostile cervix' which killed the inserted sperm. It seemed very likely to me that she had a deep issue around forgiveness of men which was being reflected in her body. As we talked together, she mentioned that her early relationships had been with men. When she was 20 years old, she had been raped and this had left a scar upon her mind. In one of her relationships she had become pregnant and had the pregnancy terminated.

We began the session with relaxation prior to focusing on Jane's feelings around men. When I suggested she work with forgiving the men who had caused her pain, she experienced strong anger. She felt this anger in her hands, legs and stomach area. At the same time, she experienced a headache. We worked with acceptance of what was happening, both of us asking for help. To her surprise, memories and feelings in connection with her abortion, which she had repressed, began to surface. Jane thought that she had healed this issue but the awakened memories were intense. At one point she began to crawl around the room like a baby. She felt she was giving the aborted child the life she had denied it.

The guilt she was now experiencing was intense and she saw it symbolised in the form of a vulture. I encouraged her not to be fearful of it and to try and accept it. Jane reported that it gradually dissolved as she watched it with love and acceptance. This was followed by a dramatic insight and Jane announced, 'I can conceive — I've forgotten this!' In her imagination she saw this energy of conception flow into her womb and a darkness leave it. She felt this symbolised her forgiveness of herself. At the end of the session, Jane wanted to give me a hug but was apprehensive due to her ambivalence towards me as a man. She cautiously held me for a short while and felt pleased she was able to touch a man again. The following day she reported experiencing some pain in her lower abdominal area which I took as a positive sign that something was changing for her. She also told me that she was practising hugging men in her imagination.

A few months later I received a letter from her. She was undergoing artificial insemination again and had arranged to meet the donor of the sperm and had gone out for a meal with him. Jane had realised her need to release her hatred of men, feeling this was reflected in her hostile cervix. She finished the letter by informing me that she was now pregnant and later sent me a photo of herself and her partner with their new baby.

The *Psychotherapy* pamphlet teaches that there is a correlation between the form of sickness in the body and the form of unforgiveness in the mind.

> *Sickness takes many forms, and so does unforgiveness. The forms of one but reproduce the forms of the other, for they are the same illusion. So closely is one translated into the other, that a careful study of the form a sickness takes will point clearly to the form of unforgiveness that it represents. Yet seeing this will not effect a cure. That is achieved by only one recognition; that only forgiveness heals an unforgiveness, and only an unforgiveness can possibly give rise to sickness of any kind. This realisation is the final goal of psychotherapy.*
>
> (P13; P-2.VI.5,6:1)

It can be very helpful for some people to see this connection between the mind and body. However, if this insight is not followed by forgiveness, healing will not result. I have witnessed people discovering a painful suppressed memory only to use it as evidence to support their attack upon the person deemed responsible. The ego is always telling us that our present problems are due to events in the past and that we are justified in feeling the way we do now. The Holy Spirit tells us that the past does not exist, for only the present moment is real, and the distress we are feeling now is due to a decision we are making in the present. Our decision to remain a justified victim means we do not have to face the fact that we are responsible for everything we feel. No one can take our peace away from us, only ourself. It is as if each morning we wake up and switch on an internal tape recorder which plays to us all the painful memories of our past. Each day we review this tape and our feeling of being a victim is reinforced. It is difficult to see that it is our decision in the present moment which maintains our sickness and not our past history of trauma and abuse. This constant replaying of the past makes our ego seem very real and blocks the awareness of the Holy Spirit from our mind. As the Course states, 'All forms of sickness, even unto death, are physical expressions of the fear of awakening.' (T146; T-8.IX.3:2)

Why Choose Sickness?

At first thought, it seems an insane idea that we would want to choose to be sick. The Course states that the ego sees value in pain. The pain makes the body, and thus the ego, real.

> *Sickness is isolation. For it seems to keep one self apart from all the rest, to suffer what the others do not feel. It gives the body final power to make the separation real, and keep the mind in solitary prison, split apart and held in pieces by a solid wall of sickened flesh, which it cannot surmount.*
>
> (W254; W-pI.137.2)

Lesson 136 is entitled 'Sickness is a defence against the truth'. It describes how the ego seeks to protect itself by advising us to get sick if truth comes too close to us. For example, perhaps a time has come in your life when you feel guided to end a relationship. You feel you have learned the lessons it contained and you are at peace about parting and as this will be for your highest good it must also be for your partner as well. However, your partner may not agree with this at all and greatly fears losing you. The opportunity to grow that is now being offered is seen as a threat and your partner may choose sickness as 'a defence against the truth'. The focus is abruptly shifted to the effect (the body) and away from the cause (the mind). The problem is now seen elsewhere and the 'threat' of spiritual growth has been removed.The ego of your partner would also counsel that the sickness is caused by something or someone in the world. In this example, you will be the obvious first choice!

Our language is full of statements indicating that we are not guilty of creating our own pain, but others are. We are telling God that they deserve to be punished and not us. For example 'You make me feel sick', 'You get up my nose', 'Get off my back', 'You are a pain in the backside' are common statements designed to pin the guilt on someone else. The following passage from the Course powerfully portrays our ego's need to appear an innocent victim of causes outside our mind.

> *A sick and suffering you but represents your brother's guilt; the witness that you send lest he forget the injuries he gave, from which you swear he never will escape. This sick and sorry picture you accept, if only it can serve to punish him. The sick are merciless to everyone, and in contagion do they seek to kill. Death seems an easy price, if they can say, 'Behold me, brother, at your hand I die.' For sickness is the witness to his guilt, and death would prove his errors must be sins. Sickness is but a 'little' death; a form of vengeance not yet total.*
>
> (T525f; T-27.I.4:3-8)

The content of this paragraph is also related to a later section in the Text entitled 'Self Concept Versus Self' (T610; T-31.V) which describes the two faces we cultivate towards the world. We create these faces as we grow up and they bear no resemblance to our Christ nature. The first is a public face of innocence which is easily upset by what it sees as injustice, pain and sickness in the world. We identify strongly with this concept of ourself for it

'Sickness is a Defence Against the Truth'
(Title of Lesson 136)

Sickness is a decision. It is not a thing that happens to you, quite unsought, which makes you weak and brings you suffering. It is a choice you make, a plan you lay, when for an instant truth arises in your own deluded mind, and all your world appears to totter and prepares to fall. Now are you sick, that truth may go away and threaten your establishments no more.   W 251; W-pI.136.7

Fig 4.3

conceals the guilt of what lies deeper within us. This face '. . . believes that it is good within an evil world'. (T610;T-31.V.2:9) Although it does not believe it is right to attack another, if the situation 'demands it' the face of innocence will attack in self-defence. This face fails to realise that situations cannot provoke attack but only uncover the hate that already resides in our mind.

Beneath this face of the innocent victim is the hidden face of the victimiser. We are careful not to look at this second face, which is hidden deeply within us. It proclaims '. . . I am the thing you made of me, and as you look at me, you stand condemned because of what I am.' (T611;T-31.V.5:3) This is the face that needs to find people and situations onto which it can project its guilt and thus maintain its innocence. To the ego anyone is suitable for projecting its hidden guilt onto.

While the cause of our guilt is looked for in the world, we shall never question the insanity of the ego's thought system. This is why sickness is so useful to the ego. Even though we are not consciously aware of it, when we become sick, the second face will always be pointing a finger at someone and accusing them of causing the sickness. This face wants to see disasters, aggression, accidents in the world so it will feel justified in feeling an innocent victim. A story related to me by a friend graphically illustrates this.

Sally has travelled widely for many years. Each time she flies by air, she feels terrified when there is turbulence, even if the turbulence is minor. She had sought counselling in a variety of ways to work with this problem over the years. She felt she was at a point of desperation as her fear of air turbulence had steadily grown worse. Sally studies the Course and this time during a flight when there was turbulence, she turned deeply within herself and asked Jesus to help her to understand why she was so afraid. The answer came instantly and very clearly:

'You want this plane to crash — that is how strong the victim part of you is.' Sally said the instant she heard this answer she knew it was true. She still experiences fear when flying and says that she is aware she is not yet ready to let it go but she now understands that she is using this fear to keep the love of Jesus away from her.

This desire to be a victim only increases our guilt further and reinforces our belief in the ego. The Course tells us that we would willingly choose to die from an illness in the hope that we could make another feel guilty. There are no lengths our ego will not go to so we may appear innocent at someone else's expense. The Holy Spirit's response to this insanity is to ask, 'Do you prefer that you be right or happy?' (T573; T-29.VII.1:9) To be right is to make the ego's thought of separation real and suffer the consequences of feeling alone and afraid. To be wrong is to question our belief in being an innocent victim and to start to look, with the Holy Spirit's help, at the illusions in our mind.

Although we try very hard to get rid of our sense of guilt by finding others onto whom to project it, deep inside us we don't fully believe this will work; eventually God will find us and exact due and justified punishment for our sins. Once again the ego tells us that there is an advantage in getting sick, for we can use it to protect ourselves from God's full anger, for as the Course states, 'The ego believes that by punishing itself it will mitigate the punishment of God.' (T78; T-5.V.5:6) We are telling God that we know we are sinners and we will punish ourselves by accepting only a little happiness into our lives and by getting sick. In this way we hope God will be satisfied with our penance and not seek to punish us, for His punishment would destroy us.

From the Holy Spirit's perspective, all this is but the deluded thinking of people experiencing nightmares. No sins have been committed, for nothing has really happened in our silly dream of separation. Although it all seems painfully real to us, the Holy Spirit has another perspective to offer which we shall explore in the following chapters.

Any desire for spiritual growth must be attacked by our ego, for it knows no other method of response. It seeks to save itself by warning us that to go that way is dangerous and will eventually lead to our destruction. We want to return home to God but the ego tells us this is impossible, for we have destroyed our home and left an angry God behind. Jesus's story of the prodigal son illustrates this well and is the story of all of us. We are tired of living in the pigsty but fear to go home. When we do pluck up courage and return home, we find a banquet awaiting us and a loving Father.

The following story demonstrates the fear and resistance we experience as we walk along the spiritual path, and the help that is always there for us.

It was David's first visit to the Findhorn Foundation and he had enrolled for the Experience Week programme. This programme introduces the Foundation to newcomers and includes an afternoon of group games and exercises. In one of the exercises the group splits into pairs who take turns to slowly unfold their partner who lies tightly curled up on the floor. It can be a very moving experience to allow someone to gently and lovingly unfold you from a protected and defensive posture. In David's case, he felt a sensation in his pelvic area as if some energy that had been long locked away was being released. When this force reached his stomach, he decided to stop the process and the energy remained locked there.

Two weeks after this event David came to talk to me. He told me he had felt stuck ever since that exercise. He said it was like being constipated and he knew he had blocked something in himself at that moment. It reminded him of a deeper feeling that he carried, where he felt blocked and inhibited in his life in general. David was about 18 years old with a sensitive and caring nature. As he talked, I sensed that some part of him was holding back from living his life fully. He was ambivalent about being here on the planet and living purposefully. We moved into a healing session and, as we worked with relaxation, he spontaneously returned to the tight, curled-up foetal position he had adopted in the exercise two weeks before. He told me he had regressed to his birth. As he re-experienced the moment of birth, he recognised an intense resistance to coming here. He had decided there and then that he would resist this world and what it stood for.

David had not seen that he had fallen into the trap of 'making the error real' and that he was listening to the voice of his ego. He was willing to abandon the purpose of his new life and the lessons he had elected to learn in defiance of what he perceived as a hard and cruel world. David was afraid of opening to this experience and decided to try and protect his sensitive nature by psychologically closing himself down. I could readily understand his experience, for I empathised with much of what he said.

The *Psychotherapy: Purpose, Process and Practice* pamphlet points out that the therapist draws the clients who are needed to heal the therapist, for both will be working with the same issues albeit in different forms (see the section in the pamphlet on 'The Ideal Patient-Therapist Relationship').

David then said a presence had appeared which counselled him to change his mind and do what he had come to do. He was told that just as he had blocked himself at his birth, so too had he repeated this experience two weeks ago in the unfolding exercise. Now David was ready to let go and trust God's will for him. As he relaxed his tight control, he immediately began to experience the blocked energy moving upwards through his body. He experienced feeling very much looser in his body, especially in his legs. At this point be began to cry. After the session, we went for a walk together. We were both aware of a change in him. He felt more alive, energised and unguarded.

The acceptance of sickness as a decision of the mind, for a purpose for which it would use the body, is the basis of healing. And this is so for healing in all forms. A patient decides that this is so, and he recovers. If he decides against recovery, he will not be healed. Who is the physician? Only the mind of the patient himself. The outcome is what he decides that it is. Special agents (for example pills, doctors, remedies) seem to be ministering to him, yet they but give form to his desires. And it is this they do, and nothing else. They are not actually needed at all. The patient could merely rise up without their aid and say, 'I have no use for this.' There is no form of sickness that would not be cured at once.

(M17; M-5.II.2)

God does not forgive because He has never condemned. And there must be condemnation before forgiveness is necessary. Forgiveness is the great need of the world, but that is because it is a world of illusions. Those who forgive are thus releasing themselves from illusions, while those who withhold forgiveness are binding themselves to them. As you condemn only yourself, so you forgive only yourself.

from *A Course in Miracles* (W73: W-pI.46.1)

Chapter Five

Healing Ourselves

If we decide to follow the ego's advice to get ill, we shall, in the next moment, deny having made that decision. I can clearly remember a time when I became conscious of the choice I had to become sick or not.

Whilst talking with a group of people one day, I noticed the first symptoms of a cold. As I thought to myself that I should go and take some medicine, I became aware of a 'voice' saying to me, 'Careful! If you do that, you might lose your cold.' It was amazing for me to realise that part of me wanted that cold. I could also see the 'advantages' of being sick. I could imagine myself tucked up in bed with a pile of my favourite books which I never found the time to read. It would also give me an opportunity to take a rest from what I considered a heavy workload. I decided I wanted to make a conscious decision about whether to be sick or well. Taking out my diary, I looked at my appointments over the next few days. I wanted to keep these appointments instead of going to bed, even though my favourite books were a great draw! Over the next few days, I had a few mild cold symptoms which did not interfere with my work. In the language of the Course, I had chosen a miracle. This enabled me to drop the ego's thought system which portrayed me as a victim of circumstances and instead view the situation through the eyes of the Holy Spirit and forgive myself. Figure 5.1 illustrates how the decision maker always has a choice in how to view the world.

We always 'look inside' our mind first and then project what we find onto the circumstances of the world. To forgive ourself and others, we need to choose to look with the Holy Spirit's thought system and not the ego's.

'Projection Makes Perception'

'The world we see merely reflects our own internal frame of reference — the dominant ideas, wishes and emotions in our minds. "Projection makes perception." We look inside first, decide the kind of world we want to see and then project that world outside, making it the truth as we see it. We make it true by our interpretations of what it is we are seeing . . . .' (contd. below)

Decision
Maker

'Projection makes perception'

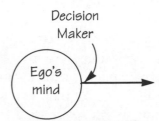

The ego's world of victims
and victimisers

'If we are using perception to justify our own mistakes — our anger, our impulses to attack, our lack of love in whatever form it may take — we will see a world of evil, destruction, malice, envy and despair . . . .'
(contd. below)

Decision
Maker

'Projection makes perception'

The Holy Spirit's world of people extending love or asking for it.

'All this we must learn to forgive, not because we are being "good" and "charitable", but because what we are seeing is not true. We have distorted the world by our twisted defences, and are therefore seeing what is not there. As we learn to recognise our perceptual errors, we also learn to look past them or "forgive" them. At the same time we are forgiving ourselves, looking past our distorted self concepts to the Self that God created in us and as us.'
Preface, 'What It Says', A Course in Miracles

Fig 5.1

One night shortly before going to sleep, Salice and I had an argument. My ego told me I had been unfairly treated and I should separate from her by not communicating. Salice's ego had apparently given her the same advice, for neither of us was now talking to the other! I got out of bed and went to the bathroom. I saw a pack of Workbook Lesson cards and felt the impulse to take one. The title of the Lesson was 'I could see peace instead of this'. (Lesson 34) The significance of the Lesson was not lost on me and simultaneously another line from the Course came into my mind: 'Do you prefer to be right or happy?' (T573; T29.VII.1:9) For a moment I considered my two options and then said to myself, 'I'd rather be right' and put the Lesson card down again. Feeling miserable but justified in my pain, I returned silently to bed and fell asleep.

In the morning I woke up still feeling separated from Salice, as she did from me. I returned to the bathroom and remembered picking up the Lesson card from the night before. Out of curiosity I read the title again, 'I could see peace instead of this', and remembered the choice I had to be right or happy. I became still for a moment and this time I chose to be happy. I felt the impulse to share what was happening to me with Salice. She was sitting quietly at the table and as I sat down next to her I said, 'I want to let you know that I'm not handling my side of this dispute very well.' At this statement Salice began to cry and we began to share honestly with each other how we had been feeling.

Through this process we were able to understand each other's fear and found ourselves quickly moving into a state of mutual openness, care and affection. In the language of the Course, we had joined and felt at peace. At these moments I always wonder why I choose to be right and not happy. However, I am also aware that it is taking me a shorter time to forgive than it has done in the past.

What would upset me for days may only last a few hours now. I am also aware that some issues which triggered pain in me in the past no longer affect me. Progress on the spiritual path may be measured by how much of the day is spent listening to the ego compared to the voice of the Holy Spirit.

Eventually, only the Holy Spirit will fill our mind and then there will be no more temptation or choice, for there will not be two voices to choose between. The decision maker will have disappeared with the ego, and the Holy Spirit will fill our mind with God's love and wisdom. We shall simply know what to do from moment to moment. The Course describes this state of existence as being in the real world and this is the goal of the Course. To achieve this goal we must practise forgiveness over and over until we at last see there is nothing to forgive.

> *Forgive the world, and you will understand that everything that God created cannot have an end, and nothing He did not create is real. In this one sentence is our course explained. In this one sentence is our practising given its one direction. And in this one sentence is the Holy Spirit's whole curriculum specified exactly as it is.*
>
> (M50; M-20.5:7-10)

How Do I Forgive?

> *It is impossible to forgive another, for it is only your sins you see in him. You want to see them there, and not in you. That is why forgiveness of another is an illusion.*
>
> (S10; S-2.I.4:2-4)

We can only begin the process of forgiveness when we start to realise how much alike we are to the person we wish to forgive. When we cannot forgive someone, it is because we cannot forgive ourselves for the same problem, albeit in another form. For example, a woman may dislike her husband's aggressive outbursts of anger, whilst she may never exhibit such outbursts herself. However, her anger will be just as strong as his but will be found in a different form. For instance, when she feels angry she may withdraw herself and cut off from people emotionally, successfully suppressing her anger. Or her anger may be expressed aggressively when she is alone. A common example for many people is when they are driving a car and someone changes lanes or stops suddenly. Anger can well up in us and in the safety and privacy of the car we may yell or swear angrily at the other driver. The woman dislikes her husband's anger because it mirrors her own which she has not forgiven in herself.

Forgiveness recognises that what we thought was done to us, we truly did to ourselves, for only we can deprive ourselves of the peace of God. As the Course teaches, we forgive others for what they have not done to us, not for what they did, and true forgiveness recognises an attack as a call for love. Forgiveness is thus a shift in perception. Our only problem is the belief in separation from God; our only healing is by joining with each other through forgiveness.

The Three Stages of Forgiveness

Kenneth Wapnick has identified in the Course three stages or steps on the path of forgiveness which I find helpful in understanding the nature of true forgiveness. I have used these steps as the basis for the following discussion on forgiveness.

Firstly we must take back the projections which we have made onto the world and take responsibility for our own pain. See Figure 5.2.

We must stop pointing our finger at people and situations and accusing them of hurting us and see that they are mirroring to us the areas we have not healed and forgiven

The First Stage of Forgiveness

Fig 5.2

in ourself. In fact these people and situations merit our thanks for showing us what is in our unconscious mind. Without them we would not see the forces that drive us.

The secret of salvation is but this: That you are doing this unto yourself. No matter what the form of the attack, this

still is true. Whoever takes the role of enemy and of attacker,
still is this the truth. Whatever seems to be the cause of any
pain and suffering you feel, this is still true. For you would
not react at all to figures in a dream you knew that you were
dreaming. Let them be as hateful and as vicious as they may,
they could have no effect on you unless you failed to recog-
nise it is your dream.

(T545; T-27.VIII.10)

Our attacks are not limited to people who are behav-
ing inappropriately and obviously acting from their ego.
We are also capable of attacking people who have done
nothing to us. I recently watched a television documentary about the life of Mao Tse Tung. During the period of
his cultural revolution he encouraged the working classes
to seek out and persecute authority figures. In one particular village the people experienced a problem carrying
out Mao's command as they had already killed the landlord several years earlier. The programme mentioned that
over a million landlords had been killed by the peasants
at the beginning of Mao's rule in China. They remembered, however, that the landlord had a son. Although he
did not hold any office of power or authority in the village, and lived as one of them, they sought him out and
tortured him to death.

This story clearly illustrates the need of our ego to find
fault outside ourself. We want to find sin in the world so
we have something onto which we can hook our projections. If we looked fully at the insanity of the ego's thought
system, we would no longer follow it. The ego is well
aware that its continuity depends on us not looking deeply into our mind and it tells us to look in the world for the
cause of our distress. The Course reminds us that 'to the
ego, the guiltless are guilty'. (T224; T-13.II.4:2) To usurp
God's power, break up Heaven and create an alternative
to God's creation is a sin, and we should feel guilty. If, like
Jesus, we don't feel guilty, we are invalidating the ego and

telling it that its creation is an illusion. This is the greatest sin we can commit against the ego and warrants death in its eyes. That is why Jesus was killed, although he had harmed no one.

The ego encourages us to attack everyone, whether they have attacked us or not. We need to see sin in the world so we don't have to confront the ego's thought system in our own mind. This is why our newspapers and television news programmes are largely filled with disturbing news. We want to read it and see it so we can say, 'They are the wicked ones, not me. They deserve God's punishment, not me. They are the cause of the pain in the world, not me.'

As we actively seek for enemies outside ourself, we simultaneously strengthen the guilt within our mind and so the ego's vicious circle of guilt and attack is complete. This trap is so hard to break free from that without the Holy Spirit's help we could never do it. Before the Holy Spirit can heal our mind, we must first discover what it is that needs healing. If we believe the problem lies in the world instead of in our mind, the Holy Spirit can do nothing to help us.

When we realise that there is no one or nothing to blame 'out there' and that the problem lies within us, we usually fall into the trap of feeling guilty. This is because we make a decision to listen to the counsel of our ego which has a very low opinion of us. Our ego tells us we should feel guilty for our sins, for in this way we will take the world of separation seriously. It is very easy to fall into the ego's trap of judgement. Guilt always demands punishment and this prevents us from releasing our pain. Our ego does not care if we blame the world or ourself for our unhappiness. Either way we are reinforcing our belief in the ego's thought system and its survival is all that it cares about.

During this second stage of forgiveness (Figure 5.3) we begin to realise how deeply attached we are to our guilt.

The Second Stage of Forgiveness

Fig 5.3

It appears to be a sacrifice not to feel justified in being a victim and the desire is to hold on to our anger, jealousy or greed.

Although guilt is painful, it is what we are familiar with and we prefer it to the increase in self-responsibility we know will come to us when we lose our attachment to being a victim. We can now choose to decide that guilt no longer serves us and that we would like it to be undone. As we have so identified with our false ego-self, we do not know how to undo our guilt. As an example, let's imagine a couple who are having an issue around jealousy.

The wife is upset with her husband because of his jealous nature. He denies that he is jealous, saying that what she sees as emotional outbursts are only his feelings of love for her. Although his wife is often upset by his possessiveness, she unconsciously approves of it and translates his need of her as love. One day the husband realises that his own thoughts of insecurity are producing his jealous feelings and that his wife is not to blame for his unhappiness. He also realises that if he forgives himself and lets his jealousy go, his wife might become so threatened at losing his 'love' that the relationship might end. At this point his ego will rush in and guide him to keep his jealousy or he might lose everything.

The husband is now caught in a difficult situation, for to allow his jealousy to go appears to him as a sacrifice. Thus this second stage of forgiveness can be more difficult to accomplish than the insight needed in the first stage. If, however, he chooses to listen to the Holy Spirit, he will realise that the healing of his jealous nature will take him further along the path of peace. Perhaps his wife will leave him but he has prepared the way to be with people who do not mistake jealousy for love.

Our little willingness to change, to shift our perception, opens the way for the third stage of forgiveness. In this final stage our guilt is undone by the Holy Spirit as we allow His light and peace to shine away our guilt. The following prayer from the Course contains within it the three stages of forgiveness. The Course urges us to use it whenever we are not joyous.

> *I must have decided wrongly, because I am not at peace.*
> *I made the decision myself, but I can also decide otherwise.*
> *I want to decide otherwise, because I want to be at peace.*
> *I do not feel guilty, because the Holy Spirit will undo all the consequences of my wrong decision if I will let Him.*
> *I choose to let Him, by allowing Him to decide for God for me.*

(T83; T-5.VII.6:7-11)

The Third Stage of Forgiveness

The Holy Spirit asks of you but this: bring to Him every secret you have locked away from Him. Open every door to Him, and bid Him enter the darkness and lighten it away. At your request He enters gladly. He brings the light to the darkness if you make the darkness open to him.
T268; T-14.VII.6:1-4

Fig 5.4

The first two sentences of the above prayer describe the first step of forgiveness and how we must take responsibility for the way we feel. If our peace has gone, it is because we have given it away and not because it has been taken from us. The third sentence of the quotation reflects the second step of forgiveness, when the decision is taken to see our sins as errors which can be corrected. In this step we stop listening to our ego's counsel that we are guilty and deserving of punishment and choose instead to have our errors healed. The last sentence of the quotation describes how the Holy Spirit will come to heal our mind once we have invited Him in. See Figure 5.4

The first two steps of this forgiveness process are taken by us. In the first step, we take our projections back and stop judging the world. In the second step, we stop judging ourselves and ask for help. This now makes way for the third step that is taken by the Holy Spirit. We have invited His light into the darkness of our guilt and He shines it away by His very presence, just as a dark room cannot remain dark when light is brought into it. In this analogy we can recognise that light is real, and that darkness is simply the absence of light. We cannot bring a 'lamp of darkness' into a lighted room and make the room dark but we can bring a light into a darkened room and make it light.

Whenever we agree to invite the Holy Spirit into our mind, the ego's world of darkness must disappear into the nothingness that it really is. It is often difficult to remember that there is always the Holy Spirit's love waiting to respond to any genuine call for help. It is easy for us to fall into the trap that we have to sort out all our problems ourselves. Our ego firmly believes it knows how to do this. In contrast, the Course tells us that the ego only knows how to create problems and we must get help from outside its thought system if we are to experience peace. The third step of forgiveness reminds us that we can only be helped by the Holy Spirit. Our only responsibility is to understand that we have given our peace away and that the errors in our thinking can be corrected by the Holy Spirit, once we invite Him in.

An experience I had some time ago illustrates the above three stages of forgiveness. I had been experiencing a pain in my chest for two days. It was not unfamiliar to me as I had experienced this feeling many times before in my life. It would come when I perceived myself as being unfairly treated and sometimes would last up to three days. The pain weighed me down with an intense feeling of sadness and heaviness. As I lay on my bed wondering why I was going through this all again I decided to look honestly at the 'advantages' I knew I must be gaining for holding on to the pain.

My new willingness to look at myself soon revealed the sweet pleasure of self-pity and the desire to close my heart so I would not be expected to give so much to others. I felt inside that I no longer wanted to carry this pain around and was ready to release it and accept the increase in self-responsibility which now did not seem like a sacrifice. It was not serving me any more and I could give it away. I brought my awareness and acceptance to the heart area and offered the pain to the Holy Spirit. I asked Him to take it, knowing that it would give Him joy to receive it. To my own astonishment the pain disappeared in under a minute. In fact I worried that the pain would return at any moment. But it didn't, nor have I suffered such long periods of chest pain again.

I remember seeing advertisements on billboards saying, 'Cast your burdens on the Lord'. I thought this an impossible idea and knew it could not work. It was surely up to me to sort everything out in my life. As my perception and awareness of the Holy Spirit grew, I realised what love He must have for us and that He views our activities as a mother would her child having a nightmare.

She would not condemn the content of her child's nightmare but seek gentle ways of waking the child up. How much more then would God love to take away our self-created nightmares if only we would let Him. To practise forgiveness we must first stop judging the world and then stop judging ourselves. As we do this, our ego defences are lowered and automatically the love and the light of the Holy Spirit will shine our guilt away.

When we allow ourself to wake up from our ego nightmares by practising forgiveness, we shall discover that we are still as God created us, perfect and eternal, and that nothing can harm us. What then will there be to forgive? As the Course says: 'And that in complete forgiveness, in which you recognise that there is nothing to forgive, you are absolved completely.' (T298; T-15.VIII. 1:7) This realisation that forgiveness is an illusion does not come until the end of the process of forgiveness. Whilst we believe we are separated from God, forgiveness is a helpful illusion that will awaken us from all illusions.

Our Resistance to Forgiveness

It is often thought by people new to studying *A Course in Miracles* that their lives will become more peaceful as they begin to practise its teachings. However this does not always follow. In fact things may seem to get worse, not better. Before practising the principles of the Course, they will probably have heeded the ego's counsel and denied the guilt they feel and projected it onto others. Now they attempt to bring their unconscious mind to consciousness, which starts the process of undoing denial, bringing their guilt to the light of the Holy Spirit to be forgiven. To become aware of the ego's darkness in the mind is not an easy process.

The principles of forgiveness as described in the Course are relatively simple to understand and bring us great rewards if we apply them. It is also true that most of us find it very difficult to own our pain and ask for help. To help us understand why this is so, the Course goes to great lengths to show how subtle and devious the ego really is. We are largely unconscious of the way it operates owing to the wall of denial we have constructed. The Course encourages us to look behind that wall and learn to laugh gently at what we find there.

As we practise forgiveness, at the same time we shall be lessening the importance we have given to the ego. Having identified so strongly with the ego's thought system, it seems as if we are sacrificing something very dear to us. As we bring our darkness (illusions) to the light (truth) the Course states that we will experience 'periods of unsettling'. These are times of discomfort and anxiety that we must inevitably feel in the process of shifting from the ego's thought system (wrong-mindedness) to the Holy Spirit's thought system (right-mindedness).

> *First, they (God's Teachers) must go through what might be called 'a period of undoing'. This need not be painful, but it usually is so experienced. It seems as if things are being taken away, and it is rarely understood initially that their lack of value is merely being recognised.*
>
> (M8; M-4.I.3:1-3)

This quotation is taken from a section which describes the six stages in the development of trust. Jesus cautions us that four of these stages are normally experienced as difficult and thus we should not underestimate the challenges involved in spiritual growth.

It would be helpful to take a closer look at our investment in the ego and what it seems to offer us. As we start to question the 'gifts' it holds out to us, our practice of forgiveness will become easier. Our ego will tell us that we are the most important person in the world. We have special needs which must be fulfilled and we feel justified in using whatever means are necessary to achieve this. The Course tells us that the source of this justification comes from an insane belief stored in our unconscious mind. This belief states that we are lacking the things we need because they have been stolen from us. (See 'The Laws of Chaos' in Chapter 23 of the Text) This thought justifies the use of any means to get back what we feel is rightfully ours in the first place. Forgiveness teaches the opposite of this and states that we have given away our remembrance of our spiritual reality in exchange for the experience of individual uniqueness — the need to feel special and different from others.

When we decided to forget our true state of unity within the One Mind of God, competition and judgement had to follow. To maintain a sense of individuality we must continually compare ourselves to others and look for differences. If we meet someone who seems better than us in some way, then we must make them into our enemy or put them onto a pedestal and appear to look up to them. However, at a deeper level of our mind we will hate them for being better than us. The Course states: 'Only the special could have enemies, for they are different and not the same. And difference of any kind imposes orders of reality, and a need to judge that cannot be escaped.' (T465; T-24.I.3:5-6) When we come across someone whom we judge as inferior, there will be a desire to keep this person the way they are so we may appear superior by contrast. The Course describes this dynamic as follows:

> *Against the littleness you see in him you stand as tall and stately, clean and honest, pure and unsullied by comparison with what you see. Nor do you understand it is yourself that you diminish thus.*
>
> (T466f; T-24.II.1:6-7)

This quotation reminds us that when we compare and attack our brothers we are also attacking ourself. Our attacks are always centred on another's body or their behaviour and thus our belief in the reality of the body is strengthened and our awareness of spirit is weakened.

The Course states: 'You would oppose this course because it teaches you you and your brother are alike.' (T466;T-24.I.8:6) Forgiveness teaches us that our egos are all the same, as is our Christ nature. This is the last thing our ego wants to hear. For the ego to retain its desire for specialness, it must perceive differences between itself and others. If someone goes to a party, the last thing they want to find is someone else wearing the same outfit as them.

Our original desire to be separate and different from God is perpetuated in our continuing desire to be separate from others. Forgiveness would undo this thought and eventually return to our awareness our oneness with each other and God. This is perceived by our ego as an act of treachery which deserves punishment. To welcome the state of unity back into our awareness means the death of the ego and this it must fight with all its resources.

> *The ego is deceived by everything you do, especially when you respond to the Holy Spirit, because at such times its confusion increases. The ego is, therefore, particularly likely to attack you when you react lovingly, because it has evaluated you as unloving and you are going against its judgement. The ego will attack your motives as soon as they become clearly out of accord with its perception of you. This is when it will shift abruptly from suspiciousness to viciousness, since its uncertainty is increased.*

> (T164; T-9.VII.4:4-7)

We might experience a day when we feel open to the love of the Holy Spirit and feel a deep sense of peace and well-being. We may even think this state could last forever. However, we might wake the following day feeling depressed and alone and wonder why things have changed so much. To allow this shift to occur, we must be persuaded by our ego that to continue listening to the Holy Spirit is dangerous. The ego reminds us that it is safer to stay as we are as change will involve sacrifice and, even worse, there is an avenging god awaiting us at the end of our journey ready to punish us for our many sins. We are told that if we follow the path of forgiveness, we shall have to look at all the horror and darkness within our mind, and that we shall not survive this experience. The journey of forgiveness is not an easy one, but its success is guaranteed by God, for it is His will that we return to Him.

False Forgiveness

No gift of Heaven has been more misunderstood than has forgiveness. It has, in fact, become a scourge; a curse where it was meant to bless, a cruel mockery of grace, a parody upon the holy peace of God.

(S9; S-2.I.1:1-2)

The *Song of Prayer* pamphlet describes a number of false concepts about forgiveness which are called 'forgiveness-to-destroy'. (S11f; S-2.IIf) Firstly, there is what might be called the 'holier than thou' form of forgiveness. In this, the offended person adopts a posture of spiritual superiority and seeming charity and decides to 'forgive' the inferior individual who has offended him. The person is effectively saying, 'Out of the kindness of my heart I forgive you for what you have done to me, but don't do it again.' With this form of forgiveness the 'forgiver' does not see the problem is within him and loses an opportunity to heal himself of what the other person is mirroring to him.

Forgiveness-to-destroy has many forms, being a weapon of the world of form. Not all of them are obvious, and some are carefully concealed beneath what seems like charity.

(S11; S-2.II.1:1-2)

Another form of false forgiveness can be described as

that of the 'martyred saint'. In this form, a person believes
he is a sinner and deserves God's punishment, which he
accepts with apparent humility and lack of defence. However, this is a statement of belief in the ego and not in God,
for only the ego counsels us we have sinned. We may
actively seek to be martyred so we can display our 'saint-
liness' to others. However, behind an exterior of smiling
acceptance lies the anger and bitterness we feel towards
the other person. Thus the ego uses false forgiveness to
reinforce our belief in it.

A further form of 'forgiveness-to-destroy' is based on
bargaining and compromise. As long as another person
is meeting most of our ego needs, we are willing to forgive their transgressions against us. When our needs are
no longer met, there is no reason left to forgive them and
our denied hate now rises to the surface in the form of an
attack.

Holy Relationships

*As you come closer to a brother you approach me, and as
you withdraw from him I become distant to you. Salvation
is a collaborative venture. It cannot be undertaken successfully by those who disengage themselves from the Sonship,
because they are disengaging themselves from me. God will
come to you only as you will give Him to your brothers.*

(T63; T-4.VI.8:1-4)

Relationships are necessary to show us what needs healing under our barriers of denial. This is true for all forms
of relationship. Every time we come into contact with
another person we have an opportunity to look within
and forgive the illusions we hold about ourselves. Without the mirroring of others, it would be impossible to find
all the guilt we have denied. This guilt which we all carry
is buried deeply within our mind and protected by a wall
of denial. As a further defence we project what we deny

onto the world and especially onto other people.

The ego tells us that it is not we who have a problem but the people with whom we enter into some form of relationship. However, in the eyes of the Holy Spirit these very same people are our teachers, for without them it would be impossible to see what we have denied. We need something outside our closed mind to show us what is really inside it. When we are shown something we do not like about ourselves, our ego tells us to attack the other person. This is the same as throwing a brick at a mirror because we do not like the reflection we see.

In earlier times, messengers were used to convey important news to heads of government. It was not uncommon for the messenger to be executed if he brought news which was upsetting. Not wishing to take responsibility for the effects of the message upon themselves, the rulers projected the cause of their pain as an attack by the messenger. In the same way, our friends, enemies, parents, lovers, employers or children will continuously bring us messages about what we have denied about ourselves and have blamed on them instead.

Any time we feel even the slightest irritation in someone's presence, our hidden guilt is being triggered. If at that moment, instead of attacking the other person, we asked the Holy Spirit to help us find peace again, we would, in that instant, undo the ego's thought system. There would be a shift from desiring a special hate relationship to desiring a holy relationship. The other person has now become our teacher and no longer our enemy.

Without other people acting as mirrors to what is locked away in our unconscious mind, we would find it very difficult to uncover all that needs forgiving in ourselves. As we take responsibility for our own feelings, we begin to see, with the Holy Spirit's help, that what disturbs us in the world is nothing but a reflection of what disturbs us about ourself.

If our attitude to another person can be one of self-responsibility, truth, forgiveness, joining, defencelessness and shared interest (i.e. awaking from the dream of separation), then we have created what the Course calls a holy relationship. We have invited the Holy Spirit into our relationship. This is a very difficult attitude to maintain, for it is opposite to that advised by the ego. However, we can have the goal of a holy relationship, accepting that many times we will take our ego's advice and attack again.

This is especially true at the start of a holy relationship when the ego tries to convince us to return to the special relationship of love or hate that we once had. As the goal of our relationship begins to shift from special to holy, it will often feel that we have lost something important. 'Where has the romance and passion gone?' a lover may exclaim. A son or daughter may say, 'My parents were everything to me but now they no longer seem so special!' As our desire to have special people in our lives begins to disappear, the ego warns us to return to what once seemed to work for us.

> *The holy relationship, a major step toward the perception of the real world, is learned. It is the old, unholy relationship, transformed and seen anew . . . the only difficult phase is the beginning. For here, the goal of the relationship is abruptly shifted to the exact opposite of what it was . . . This is accomplished very rapidly, but it makes the relationship seem disturbed, disjunctive and even quite distressing . . . Many relationships have been broken off at this point, and the pursuit of the old goal re-established in another relationship . . . You will find many opportunities to blame your brother for the 'failure' of your relationship, for it will seem at times to have no purpose. A sense of aimlessness will come to haunt you, and to remind you of all the ways you once sought for satisfaction and thought you found it. Forget not now the misery you really found, and do not breathe life into your failing ego.*   (T337f; T362f in 2nd ed.)

Kenneth Wapnick has stressed it is important to realise that as the holy relationship is an attitude we develop towards other people, it only takes one person to have a holy relationship. What helps me recognise the truth of his statement is to imagine myself trapped alone on a desert island. Would it be impossible for me to have a holy relationship as there are no other people around? Would this opportunity for growth now be lost to me? If I realise, however, that what is important is my attitude of mind to the memories I hold about people, I realise that all the forgiveness I need to practise is still necessary. In the same way, if a person I hated suddenly died I could still achieve a holy relationship with that person if I learned to forgive myself.

Your partner may not share your spiritual path and may even be hostile towards you. However, you can still have a holy relationship with them. Learning to be at peace around an angry person will produce accelerated growth. This is not to say we must remain with anyone with whom it no longer feels right. The Holy Spirit has no concern for the form of the relationship, whether we stay together or part from each other, but is concerned with how we will best learn our lessons of forgiveness.

Jesus has a holy relationship with everyone, whether they have one with him or not. Because of this he was able to be at peace during his capture, trial and crucifixion. Even as the soldiers hammered nails into his body, he could only see sleeping Sons of God asking for his love. This he gave by not attacking them or defending himself. Knowing himself to be eternal, formless spirit and not the body, he knew he could not be attacked and therefore there was no need for defence. It is only when we identify with our body that we feel we need to defend ourself. As we come to realise our true reality and that 'nothing real can be threatened' (Intro, Text), we will experience the peace that Jesus knows.

I was once told a story that illustrated in a powerful way what forgiveness and a holy relationship really is. During the liberation of a particular concentration camp at the end of the Second World War, the allies discovered a prisoner who seemed in particularly good shape considering the conditions he had lived under. They presumed he had lived in the camp only a short while. When he told them he had been there for four years, they suspected him of collaboration with the Germans. However, when they saw how the other inmates treated him with respect, they knew there must be another explanation. They asked him for his story and this is what he told them.

During the time of the uprising of the Jews in the Warsaw ghetto, he and his wife and children were captured. The soldiers shot his family in front of him but did not shoot him. He asked to be shot as well but they refused, saying he had language skills which they could use in the concentration camp. At that moment he knew that unless he forgave them, and therefore himself, he would become like Hitler. With this act of forgiveness, he could see the fear in the soldiers and saw it as an appeal for his love. He had accepted the judgement of the Holy Spirit. During his years in the camp, he perceived no difference between the victims and the victimisers. Both groups were in fear and thus were asking for his love. He did not take sides, seeing everyone as the same. This enabled him to retain his sense of inner peace and strength by maintaining a holy relationship with all whom he met. This story also illustrates how everything in this world is neither good nor bad but simply neutral. Everything can be used by the Holy Spirit as a classroom in which to learn forgiveness, peace and joy.

You have no idea of the tremendous release and deep peace that comes from meeting yourself and your brothers totally without judgement.

(T42; T-3.VI.3:1)

When the ego tempts you to sickness do not ask the Holy Spirit to heal the body for this would merely be to accept the ego's belief that the body is the proper aim of healing. Ask rather that the Holy Spirit teach you the right perception of the body, for perception alone can be distorted. Only perception can be sick because only perception can be wrong.

from *A Course in Miracles* (T146; T-8.IX.1:5-7)

Chapter Six

Asking for Help

In our search for healing there comes a time when we realise that we can only receive help from outside our ego's thought system. The help of the Holy Spirit is always available to us but it needs to be invited in. The Holy Spirit cannot come where it is not welcome, for it will never go against our free will. To ask for help is to understand what true prayer really means.

The subject of prayer is easily misunderstood because of our identification with our ego needs. The ego gives us a shopping list of what to pray for and tells us that this will bring us happiness. Following the ego's advice, we pray for things like money, security, status, power and healing of our bodies and often we feel disappointed when our prayers are not answered. In this chapter we shall explore the difference between true and false prayer and the role of the Holy Spirit. I have been considerably helped in the writing of this chapter by Ken Wapnick's commentary on the pamphlet *The Song of Prayer* found on a nine-tape set of the same name (see Recommended Books & Tapes).

We all have a psychic ability to manifest things. Some people can draw to themselves money and material goods, others are good at getting parking places and taxis. The Bible, too, states that if we believe we will get what we pray for, we will receive it. Psychic abilities are of a neutral nature and can be used by either the ego or the Holy Spirit, but the abilities themselves do not bring the peace and joy of God into our lives.

As his awareness increases, he may well develop abilities
that seem quite startling to him. Yet nothing he can do can

compare even in the slightest with the glorious surprise of
remembering who he is.

(M59; M-25.1:4-5)

The question the Course would always encourage us
to ask is, 'What is it for?' In the hands of the ego, psychic
power is used to reinforce the seeming reality of our
world. Believing its advice that happiness can only be
found outside ourself, we use this power to attract the
forms of this world. Even if we are successful in our man-
ifestations, lasting peace and happiness are still not forthcoming and so we are forced to try and obtain something
else, or more of the same. 'Seek and do not find' (T210; T-
12.V.7:1) is the ego's dictum, and in this way we keep our
attention fixed on the world of form and away from spirit.

False and True Prayer

These forms of prayer, or asking-out-of-need, always involve
feelings of weakness and inadequacy, and could never be
made by a Son of God who knows Who he is ... True prayer
must avoid the pitfall of asking to entreat. Ask, rather, to
receive what is already given; to accept what is already there.

(S3, S1; S-1.II.2:1, S-1.I.1:6-7)

When we pray for external things to happen, whether for
ourself or others, we are implying that we know what is
the best solution. The Course points out that all we know
is how to create problems and only the Holy Spirit knows
how to solve them and return us to a state of peace. Our
ego-based prayers seek to change the circumstances of
our life so we can be happy again. If only we could get
enough money, heal our bodies or find the right partner,
we think we would be happy.

The Holy Spirit is not concerned with getting rid of our
problems but with helping us to find peace in them. Our
prayers should not be about changing the world, but

about changing our mind with regard to the world. The world will never be as we want it to be but we can learn to be at peace within it. The Holy Spirit is not concerned with the forms of this world because they are the mis-creations of our ego and thus illusory. To ask the Holy Spirit to act on a form level is to ask Him to believe in the same illusion we do. It is His task to awaken us from the illusion, not to adjust it to our liking. Everything in this world is the same to the Holy Spirit. He sees nothing as good or bad in itself, otherwise He would make the same mistake as us and 'make the error real'. He simply sees everything as a potential classroom for learning our lessons of forgiveness.

If our body becomes diseased, or we have an accident, we may be tempted to pray to the Holy Spirit to heal us. The Course reminds us, however, that we should pray to understand the right use of the body which is to be a tool of communication for the Holy Spirit (see quotation at the beginning of this chapter). This elevated perception is very difficult for us to appreciate and the Course is well aware of this. 'It takes great learning to understand that all things, events, encounters and circumstances are helpful.' (M9; M-4.I.4:5)

Our ego constantly advises us to change our circum-stances instead of learning to find peace in them. This is not to say that the Holy Spirit may not guide us to change our circumstances. However, His purpose will be to enable us to learn more about inner peace and will not entail any sacrifice — apart from the sacrifice of letting go our illusions, and this of course is often experienced as painful. The Holy Spirit is only concerned with the cause of a problem, which is a wrong perception in our mind. If we invite Him to help us at the causative level, He can create a shift of perception (a miracle) in our mind which will restore to us the peace we have lost. This is in oppo-sition to the ego's approach which is only concerned with the effect of the problem, which is seen outside our mind in the world. It is here that the ego asks us to direct our prayers for change. The Course states:

> . . . *The only meaningful prayer is for forgiveness, because those who have been forgiven have everything. Once forgiveness has been accepted, prayer in the usual sense becomes utterly meaningless. The prayer for forgiveness is nothing more than a request that you may be able to recognise what you already have.*

(T40;T-3.V.6:3-5)

If God has given us everything at our Creation, what 'gifts' of the earth can possibly compare with this? When we have completed our process of forgiveness, we shall awaken from our dream of separation and find all God's gifts of love, peace, joy and creativity waiting for us to reclaim them. The very act of praying for specifics reinforces our belief in scarcity and affirms our ego. Prayer, like forgiveness, is a process. Jesus likens it to a ladder and we must all start at the bottom. See Figure 6.1.

At the bottom of the ladder we use prayer to entreat, asking for things of this world, which only reinforces our sense of scarcity and separation. Our prayers to heal our body are also found at this level. Believing our body is our most important possession we become very concerned for its safety and health. If the motive for our prayers is to heal our body, we will reinforce the reality of the ego's world of form. The ego identifies with our body and makes it its home. If our prayers are only concerned with the well-being of our body we are reinforcing our belief in the ego. But if we pray to the Holy Spirit to show us how we can be at peace with our bodily problems, we can turn a bodily symptom into a classroom of forgiveness.

Over time the emphasis of our prayer shifts from form to qualities we desire — peace, for example. Even here the prayer for peace is affirming that we do not already possess

The Ladder of Prayer

True prayer must avoid the pitfall of asking to entreat. Ask, rather, to receive what is already given; to accept what is already there. S1; S-1.I.1:6-7

The Holy Spirit is not concerned with form, being aware only of meaning.
Text p.151; T-9.I.10:4

Prayer in its earlier forms is an illusion, because there is no need for a ladder to reach what one has never left. S4; S-1.II.8:3

It is not easy to realise that prayers for things, for status, for human love, for external 'gifts' of any kind, are always made to set up jailers and to hide from guilt. S6; S-1.III.6:1

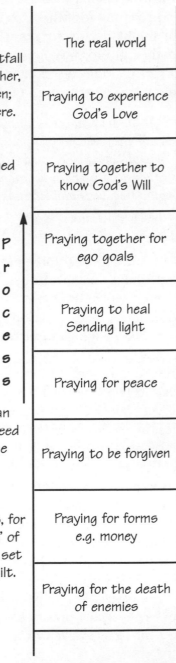

Fig 6.1

it, that God has not already given it to us. In the process of learning what true prayer is, we shall feel moved at times to pray for others, or to send them light and love. We might decide to pray for our enemies or to heal another, but to pray for one's enemies is to fall into the trap of making the error real, for there are no enemies, only mirrors to the guilt within us.

> *We said that prayer is always for yourself, and this is so. Why, then, should you pray for others at all? And if you should, how should you do it? Praying for others, if rightly understood, becomes a means for lifting your projections of guilt from your brother, and enabling you to recognise it is not he who is hurting you.*
>
> (S5; S-1.III.1:1-4)

To pray to God to heal others implies that there is a God who is unaware of the suffering of His children and through our petition we can win a special favour from Him. Thus we create a God who can be persuaded to heal some people whilst forgetting or neglecting the suffering of others. The Course teaches that God loves all his children equally and created the Holy Spirit to bring us all back to Him. Everyone has equal access to the healing power of the Holy Spirit if we would only invite His help. He is aware of everyone and does not need our petitions.

We might think that it would help to send light to another or to some trouble spot on the planet. However, this would only reinforce the reality of the ego's world of form. If we see darkness in the world it is because we see darkness in our own mind, and this is where the light is needed. As the Course states: '. . . Seek not to change the world, but choose to change your mind about the world.' (T415: T-21.Intro.1:7)

The *Psychotherapy* pamphlet does state that we need not be physically present to help others and that 'they will be sent in whatever form is most helpful; a name, a thought, a picture, an idea, or perhaps a feeling of reaching out to someone somewhere.' (P17; P-3.I.3:8) It is the Holy Spirit who 'sends' people to us to join with and not we who direct His healing ministry.

From here our prayers move to asking how to forgive ourselves so we may know that all has already been given to us by God. Finally, our prayer returns to what it once was before the separation seemed to happen — a song of love and thanks between God and His creation.

All Our Prayers are Answered

The Course tells us that all our prayers are answered but how they are answered depends on whom we pray to in the first place — the ego or the Holy Spirit. (See M 51; M-21.2,3) If we pray to the ego for things of the ego's world, we may or may not receive them depending upon our ability to manifest on a psychic level, but we will always receive the experience of the ego's world which is sin, guilt and fear. For example, we may manifest the money we think we need and temporarily feel happy, but we continue to fear that it may not be enough for our future needs, or we may lose it or have it stolen, or we feel guilty about where the money came from. In this way our prayers to the ego maintain and reinforce its presence in our mind.

Some years ago I watched a short story on television called 'The Monkey's Paw' which illustrated that we do not know our own best interests. One day a traveller knocked on the door of an elderly couple and asked them for help. In return for their kindness he gave them a gift of a monkey's paw telling them it could bestow on them three wishes. For their first wish they asked for a large sum of money. It was not long after they had made their wish that they heard another knock on their door. On opening the door they found a representative from an insurance company who told them that their son had been killed at his place of work. There had been a dreadful accident and he had got caught in a machine. He then handed the couple a cheque which was the firm's compensation for their son's death. When they opened it they found it was for the exact sum they had prayed for. Overcome by the horror of what had happened, the couple made a second wish and asked for their son to be returned to them. Soon there was another knock on the door. What they saw when they opened the door made them recoil in terror. Their son had returned but his body was horribly mangled by the accident. The parents slammed the door closed and, taking the monkey's paw for the last time, wished their son to be dead again.

If we direct our prayers towards the Holy Spirit, we shall receive his gifts of peace, joy and forgiveness. True prayer is not concerned with the world of form (effect) but with attaining peace in our mind (cause). If you find yourself at the end of a long queue waiting to buy a ticket for a bus you know will be leaving shortly, you have a choice of to whom to pray. You may ask the Holy Spirit to delay the bus or make the queue move faster, or you could ask the Holy Spirit to show you how to be at peace in this situation.

The first prayer is to the ego, for you are asking for change at the level of form. In the case of the second prayer, if it is genuinely meant, the Holy Spirit has been invited into your mind and will bring His gift of peace, which will not depend on whether you eventually catch the bus or not. It may not be for your highest good to catch that bus; you cannot know this but the Holy Spirit does.

In our desire to form a special relationship with the Holy Spirit, it is easy to fall into the trap that He does things in our lives. Figure 6.2[7] uses the analogy of a lighthouse to illustrate how the Holy Spirit acts in our lives.

[7] Figures 6.2 and 6.3 are based on an analogy used by Ken Wapnick in his tape set *The Song of Prayer*.

The Holy Spirit Does Not Do Anything
He simply reminds us of our choice for peace

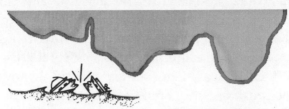

The light of the Holy Spirit is in our mind

The Voice of the Holy Spirit does not command, because it is incapable of arrogance. It does not demand, because it does not seek control. It does not overcome, because it does not attack. It merely reminds. It is compelling only because of what it reminds you of. It brings to your mind the other way, remaining quiet even in the midst of the turmoil you may make. The Voice for God is always quiet, because it speaks of peace. T70; T-5.II.7:1-7

Fig 6.2

One ship's captain feels so sure in his own knowledge of the correct course to take that he does not check to see if there is a lighthouse in the vicinity. His ship takes a dangerous course and finally goes aground and sinks. The other captain is open to receiving help and actively looks for the lighthouse and then navigates with its assistance. He changes course and proceeds safely with his journey. In both examples the lighthouse did not do anything. It did not push one ship onto the rocks because the captain would not listen to it, nor force the other ship onto a safe course to reward the captain's faith.

The quotation in Figure 6.2 tells us that the presence of the Holy Spirit's love and light in our mind is a reminder of another way of being. Whether we follow that way or not has no effect on the Holy Spirit — He just continues to shine. The Holy Spirit does not order, command or demand anything of us. Nor does He overcome the obstacles on our path. He simply reminds us that there is another way of being. If we forgive, the obstacles will no longer be there. The form of the problem may still be there — for example our car may still not start — but now we will be at peace with it. The problem never was the faulty car but the hidden guilt that was triggered in us when it failed to start. The Workbook states it this way: 'I am never upset for the reason I think.' (Lesson 5) In every situation the Holy Spirit reminds us that there is always another way of looking at a problem that will bring us peace. 'Choose again' the Course counsels us and have 'a little willingness' to invite the Holy Spirit to help us.

From our perspective it may often feel as if the Holy Spirit comes and goes in our lives. One moment we feel His presence, only to feel deserted by Him in the next. The truth is that we are the ones who decide to come close and then move away.

The Holy Spirit will, of Himself, fill every mind that so makes room for Him . . . If you cannot hear the Voice for

God, it is because you do not choose to listen. That you do listen to the voice of your ego is demonstrated by your attitudes, your feelings and your behaviour.

(T278; T-14.XI.13:6; T57; T-4.IV.1:1-2)

To feel the presence of the Holy Spirit is terrifying to our ego for it will dissolve in the Holy Spirit's presence. We feel we can only take so much love and light and then we need to return to the secure darkness of our ego. However, the light of the Holy Spirit continues to shine unaffected in our mind, awaiting with infinite patience our next call for His help. See Figure 6.3.

Summary

The *Song of Prayer* pamphlet uses the analogy of a ladder to illustrate our progression in the use of prayer. At the bottom of the ladder are prayers to entreat. Unaware we have already been given everything by God, our inherent sense of sin and guilt tells us we have something lacking in us (the scarcity principle). No longer aware of God's love for us, we translate this lack into material needs. We pray to God to give us the things we think we need — for example, money, healing for our bodies etc. We believe these things can bring us peace, forgetting that the very form of this prayer reinforces our feeling that we are lacking certain things and that the answer to our needs lies outside our mind. We notice that some people are very good at manifesting parking places, money or self-healing and think they have the secret of prayer. We forget the enormous power of our mind and that some people have learned to do this. We are tempted to think that the Holy Spirit brings these gifts, not realising 'the Holy Spirit is not concerned with form, being aware only of meaning'. (T151;T-9.I.10:4) But these psychic powers do not bring peace. We are continually tempted to pray for specific things and thus restrict the answer within the limits we have set up.

The Holy Spirit is Always Present in Our Mind

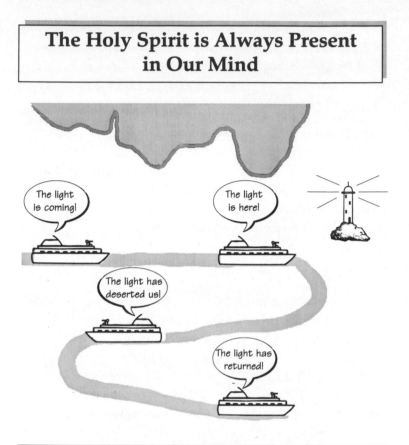

Why wait for Heaven? Those who seek the light are merely covering their eyes. The light is in them now. Enlightenment is but a recognition, not a change at all. Light is not of the world, yet you who bear the light in you are alien here as well. The light came with you from your native home, and stayed with you because it is your own. It is the only thing you bring with you from Him Who is your Source. It shines in you because it lights your home, and leads you back to where it came from and you are at home.
W347; W-pI.188.1

Fig 6.3

All our prayers are answered depending on whom we pray to. Ego-based prayers for things of this world are answered by experiences of the ego's world — some form of guilt and fear. We may actually get the form of what we pray for but in so doing we maintain our focus on externals, reinforce the world of separation and thus maintain our feelings of guilt and our belief in the ego. The Course reminds us that '. . . the only meaningful prayer is for forgiveness, because those who have been forgiven have everything'. (T40; T-3.V.6:3)

The Holy Spirit is not interested in getting rid of our problems (ego prayers) but in showing us what to do to be at peace with the challenges in our lives. As we let Him teach us to forgive, we will undo the guilt we carry which blocks us from knowing that we have everything already. At the top of the ladder of prayer we realise we have no needs and prayer turns back into the original form it had before the separation seemed to happen. This form is a song of thanks to and from our Creator, sung without thoughts, desires or needs.

I am here only to be truly helpful.
I am here to represent Him Who sent me.
I do not have to worry about what to say or
do, because He Who sent me will direct me.
I am content to be wherever He wishes
knowing He goes there with me.
I will be healed as I let Him teach me to heal.

from *A Course in Miracles* (T24; T-2.V.18:2-6)

Chapter Seven

Healing Others

Introduction

What is it that needs healing, and how is it achieved? Is it the techniques of healers which heal or are they only the forms through which healing can come? What is it that heals and is it only a certain gifted or chosen few who possess these abilities? What are the differences between the healed and the unhealed healer? This chapter will consider these questions and explore them in the light of what the Course has to say about them.

The Aim of Healing

This book began by stating that all our physical and psychological problems originate from only one problem, the belief that we are separate from each other and from God. Through the power of denial and the veil of forgetfulness which we have created about our true home, we are forced to seek outside our mind for healing. The pain in our body and psyche calls for instant relief. In this way we can get trapped into seeking help only for the symptoms of our one problem and forget to look more deeply at the cause in our mind. We seek healers to repair our damaged physical and emotional bodies and when this is done we become content for a little while until a new symptom appears.

It is not wrong to seek relief for our pain, but symptom relief is not true healing. If you have a severe headache, your attention will probably be centred on the pain and not on its cause. Taking some form of medication to ease the pain will provide an opportunity to help find the unforgiveness in the mind. We need to use these symptoms to remind us that the cause of our distress is not to be found in the world but in our decision to remain separate. As all our pain comes from separation, healing must come from joining. If we cannot find what it is that needs forgiveness, we can always begin where we are and join with those around us. By practising forgiveness from moment to moment we will undo the separation that has given rise to pain.

The true function of a healer is to remind the client, through the example and presence of the healer, that he is still as God created him. This is the way that Jesus performed his miracles. Like everyone in this world, Jesus first looked within before looking without. As he looked within he saw only the Son of God, the Christ, in his own mind. When he looked without and saw a sick person asking for healing, he could only see another Son of God, albeit a sleeping one.

As the sick person came into the presence of Jesus, he saw someone who accepted him as an equal, reminding him that he could make another choice. Until this moment, the sick person was probably surrounded by people who only focused on his bodily symptoms and thus reinforced the concept of him as an ego living in a body. The presence of Jesus reminded him that he was not an ego but still as God had created him. The very power of Jesus's light was all that was needed to shine away the sick person's darkness once he had made the decision to be whole. In that short moment, the sick person realised his true nature as the Christ and therefore had no need to defend himself with sickness. Although the person's ego had been temporarily vanquished, Jesus knew it would counter-attack at the first possible opportunity, and thus he would often counsel people to 'go and sin no more'.

To receive a miraculous cure does not guarantee it will last. It has often been observed by researchers that miracle cures are rarely permanent and the healed person often succumbs to the same or a related illness after a period of months or years. The removal of the symptoms of the sickness was not the healing, but only a by-product of the peace which had now entered the person's mind. Jesus's presence was a reminder of another way of being, a call to come home to the Father's love. We need to make the answering of this call the purpose of our life here. To be fully healed is to awaken from the dream of separation in which we are lost. As we begin to awaken and allow the presence of the Holy Spirit into our mind, we can act as a channel for His healing.

> *For this alone I need; that you will hear the words I speak, and give them to the world. You are my voice, my eyes, my feet, my hands through which I save the world.*
>
> (W322; W-pI.review V.9:2)

The above quotation makes it clear that it will not be we who heal but the love and light of Jesus or the Holy Spirit which will extend through us and into the world. Jesus has become the manifestation of the Holy Spirit in our world as he is now entirely without an ego.

Sickness or Healing is Our Choice

As sickness is our choice, so is healing. No one can make us sick and no one can heal us unless it is our decision. As the Course states, 'Healing does not come from any-one else. You must accept guidance from within.' (T134; T-8.IV.4:5-6) Even in the presence of someone like Jesus, a sick person must still choose to see themself as Jesus sees them. It is evident from the Bible that many people still preferred to listen to their own ego than his voice of love and acceptance. Healing was seen as a threat to their ego's existence and so they sought refuge in fear and sickness. The illusory realm of form was preferred to the formless realm of spirit which Jesus offered. His thought system was so alien to the ego that most people were threatened and not healed by his presence. To defend itself, the ego attacked what could destroy it.

In my own experience of working with clients, I have often noticed their ambivalence towards healing. One part of them wants to be healed, whilst another part is resisting the process. It is as if they are saying, 'Please heal me but don't change the way I think about myself or the world. Please remove my symptoms but leave my ego intact.'

> *A madman will defend his own illusions because in them he sees his own salvation. Thus, he will attack the one who tries to save him from them, believing that he is attacking him. This curious circle of attack-defence is one of the most difficult problems with which the psychotherapist must deal. In fact, this is his central task; the core of psychotherapy. The therapist is seen as one who is attacking the patient's most cherished possession; his picture of himself. And since this picture has become the patient's security as he perceives it, the therapist cannot but be seen as a real source of danger, to be attacked and even killed.*
>
> (P9; P-2.IV.9)

Progress is achieved in healing when the client begins to realise that he is not a victim of the world but only of his own thoughts. As he begins to understand this, his ego will counsel him to attack the healer, for the ego's very existence is now being threatened. To help a client return to the cause of his problem in his mind is also to bring him closer to the Holy Spirit who resides there. The ego is well aware that the sleeping Son of God, the decision maker, on finding the presence of the Holy Spirit may well decide to choose His guidance against the ego. If the healer can meet the attack of the client without defence or counter-attack, he will demonstrate that defences are not necessary and in that moment, the healer does not believe in the reality of the ego. This example will give an opportunity to the client to change his mind, to choose forgiveness instead of attack.

> *A sick person perceives himself as separate from God. Would you see him as separate from you? It is your task to heal the sense of separation that has made him sick. It is your function to recognise for him that what he believes about himself is not the truth. It is your forgiveness that must show him this. Healing is very simple.*
>
> (M54; M-22.6:5-10)

The Healed and the Unhealed Healer

Much can be learned about the nature of true healing by examining the differences which the Course describes between the healed and the unhealed healer. Jesus is an example of a healed healer because he only ever listens to the Voice of the Holy Spirit. Although very few are at this stage, whenever we allow the presence of the Holy Spirit into our mind during a healing session, then in that instant we become a healed healer. What follows is a number of contrasting pairs of statements, with explanations from these two perspectives. I shall use relevant quotations from the Course to clarify the difference further.

1a. The Unhealed Healer: 'I have special powers that others don't.'

> *Magic always sees something 'special' in the healer, which he believes he can offer as a gift to someone who does not have it. He may believe that the gift comes from God to him, but it is quite evident that he does not understand God if he thinks he has something that others lack.*
>
> (T111f; T-7.V.4:4-5)

The statement of the unhealed healer is an easy trap to fall into. The separated state produces a deep sense of inferiority which is often compensated for by acting in a superior manner. To believe you are specially gifted with the power of healing leads to a sense of ego inflation and subsequent comparison and judgement of other healers. Once again we see the ego's desire to be special and different from other people. The healer may realise that healing is not of him but through him. He must still be careful, however, not to fall into the trap that God has specially chosen him over others to bestow His gift of healing.

1b. The Healed Healer: 'I, along with everyone else, have all of God's qualities. We were all created equal. Differences in ability are only temporary.'

> *Healing perceives nothing in the healer that everyone else does not share with him.*
>
> (T111; T-7.V.4:3)

It is inconceivable to the healed healer that God could create differences amongst his children. God gave all of Himself to his Creation. The Course states that we lack only one attribute and that is the ability to create God. It is impossible for God to hold anything back from his Creation. That differences of ability exist amongst us in the world of the ego is equally clear, but this is only temporary, for one day everyone will wake up to the glory of who they really are. The Manual for Teachers describes the characteristics of advanced Teachers of God and states: 'Their specialness is, of course, only temporary; set in time as a means of leading out of time.' (M8; M-4.1:5)

2a. The Unhealed Healer: 'I want a fair exchange for the healing I have given you.'

> *The unhealed healer wants gratitude from his brothers, but he is not grateful to them. That is because he thinks he is*

giving something to them, and is not receiving something equally desirable in return.

(T112; T-7.V.7:1-2)

Thinking he possesses a special gift which his client does not, it seems only reasonable to receive some kind of payment in exchange for the healing. The healing given to the client appears to be a one way process and thus the unhealed healer feels he is owed something in return. Although money is the usual form of exchange, perhaps it will not be asked for, but something will be expected in return. Some healers will '. . . utilise the relationship merely to collect bodies to worship at their shrine, and this they regard as healing'. (P20; P3.II.9:8.) The last section of the *Psychotherapy: Purpose, Process and Practice* pamphlet examines the issue of payment. Jesus states that even the most advanced teacher of God has some earthly needs and that there is nothing wrong with receiving payment for the time expended by the healer. To this he adds the caution, 'One rule should always be observed: No one should be turned away because he cannot pay.' (P22; P3.III.6:1.)

2b. The Healed Healer: 'I lose nothing by giving, I only gain.'

Never forget you give but to yourself. Who understands what giving means must laugh at the idea of sacrifice.

(W345; W-pI.187.6:1)

You learn first that having rests on giving, and not on getting.

(T102; T-6.V.C.6:1)

The cost of giving is receiving. Either it is a penalty from which you suffer, or the happy purchase of a treasure to hold dear.

(T256; T-14.III.5:8-9)

The healed healer knows that to give love and peace to another is to recognise that it must be within himself in the first place. Thus his very giving strengthens his own recognition of what he must already possess. This is in opposition to the thinking of the world which believes that you must have less of something if you have given some of it away. The gifts of God can only increase by giving them away. Although the healer normally charges his client for his time, he is also aware that 'no one can pay for therapy, for healing is of God and He asks for nothing'. (P21; P-3.III.1:1)

The healed healer also recognises that he draws the clients whom he needs, to help heal himself.

> *The therapist sees in the patient all that he has not forgiven in himself, and is thus given another chance to look at it, open it to re-evaluation and forgive it.*
>
> (P13; P-2.VI.6:3)

There are no accidents in our lives and everything that happens to us has been agreed by us on some level, even if we are not aware of this. The healer will be learning the same lessons of forgiveness that the clients he draws to him are, albeit in other forms. Thus in each healing session the healer is given another opportunity to heal himself.

> *Who, then, is the therapist, and who is the patient? In the end, everyone is both. He who needs healing must heal . . . Each patient who comes to a therapist offers him a chance to heal himself.*
>
> (P13;P2.VII.1:1-3,7)

Knowing this, the healer understands that in every healing session he gives, the exchange is always equal, as each has the same chance to learn from the other.

3a. The Unhealed Healer: 'I need to heal the body/personality/situation of my client.'

At worse, they (therapists) but make the body real in their own minds, and having done so, seek for magic by which to heal the ills with which their minds endow it. How could such a process cure? It is ridiculous from start to finish.

(P8; P-2.IV.4:3-5)

Believing that the cause of the illness lies outside the mind of the client, the unhealed healer seeks to bring about changes on the level of form. Orthodox or alternative therapies are used on the body, and counselling and advice are given to help change the physical circumstances or situation of the client. Focusing on healing the symptoms, rather than the cause in the mind, is an example of what the Course calls magic. Magic is the attempt to change something on the wrong level — that is, on the level of effect instead of cause. The Course also states that there is nothing wrong with magic and most of us need magic, for the fear in our mind is too great to allow us to change our mind easily. If our teeth are hurting, then it is wise to go to the dentist.

The unhealed healer believes that his special techniques and forms of healing contain a certain power. There is no denying that certain techniques can relieve or heal a bodily condition and for many people, that is all they ask. However, 'false healing rests upon the body's cure, leaving the cause of illness still unchanged, ready to strike again until it brings a cruel death in seeming victory'. (S17; S-3.II.6:1)

3b. The Healed Healer: 'All sickness and suffering originates in our mind. There are no exceptions. To try and heal something other than the mind "makes the error real".'

The acceptance of sickness as a decision of the mind, for a purpose for which it would use the body, is the basis of healing. And this is so for healing in all forms. A patient decides that this is so, and he recovers. If he decides against recovery, he will not be healed. Who is the physician? Only the mind of the patient himself.

(M17; M-5.II.2:1-6)

The healed healer understands that his client's self image is based on sin, guilt and fear, and the anger and unforgiveness in his mind has been projected onto his body. It is the healer's task gently to remind the client that there is another way of looking at the world and himself and that only forgiveness can heal an unforgiveness.

4a. The Unhealed Healer: 'Although I do not feel the love of God, I know what to do to heal you.'

You do not understand how to overlook errors, or you would not make them. It would be merely further error to believe either that you do not make them, or that you can correct them without a Guide to correction. And if you do not follow this Guide, your errors will not be corrected . . . The way to undo them, therefore, is not of you but for you.

(T157; T-9.IV.2:2-4,7)

Until we open to the love of God, we have only our ego as a guide. The focus of the ego is always on the level of form and it is here that it will teach us what to do. It will tell us that we can acquire powerful techniques and practices which will heal others. These techniques may treat the body successfully, but not the unforgiveness in the mind. The unhealed healer prefers to rely on his own judgement, feeling he knows what is best for his client.

In our scientifically oriented age, many believe that research into better medicines and the development of high technology will bring a breakthrough in treating the sick. However, as soon as one disease is conquered, another rises to take its place. As long as we value sickness, we will continue to create it. We will not turn to the

Holy Spirit for His help until we accept that the only things we are good at is creating the problems and not the solutions.

4b. The Healed Healer: 'Only the love of God heals. As I join with you, the love and light of God fills our minds.'

> *A therapist does not heal; he lets healing be. He can point to darkness but he cannot bring light of himself, for light is not of him. Yet, being for him, it must also be for his patient. The Holy Spirit is the only Therapist. He makes healing clear in any situation in which He is the Guide. You can only let Him fulfil His function. He needs no help for this. He will tell you exactly what to do to help anyone He sends to you for help, and will speak to him through you if you do not interfere.*
>
> (T161; T-9.V.8:1-8)

The healed healer looks upon himself as a tool of communication for the healing love of God. His task is to stop listening to his ego so he may be guided by the Holy Spirit in what to say and do. In every healing situation, his only task is to forgive himself in the presence of the client, for this will allow the Holy Spirit to fill the healer's mind with His presence.

Whatever technique or school of thought the healer works with will be utilised by the Holy Spirit as a form to convey His Love and acceptance to the client. It is not the healer's technique which heals but the Love of God extended into the mind of the client. The loving acceptance of the healer gives the client the opportunity to 'choose again' and forgive instead of attack. The love of God, present in the healer, shows the client that his perceived sins have had no effect upon him, and thus the client has not sinned. If the client accepts this, his guilt and the resulting physical and psychological symptoms cease to exist. If the client is not ready to take this opportunity to forgive himself, the healing has still taken place. The Course explains this by saying the Holy Spirit continues to hold this gift of love until the time comes when the client is able to receive it.

5a. The Unhealed Healer: 'My client is an innocent victim of circumstances beyond his control.'

> *Listen to what the ego says, and see what it directs you to see, and it is sure that you will see yourself as tiny, vulnerable and afraid. You will experience depression, a sense of worthlessness, and feelings of impermanence and unreality. You will believe that you are helpless prey to forces far beyond your own control, and far more powerful than you.*
>
> (T425; T-21.V.2:2-5)

The unhealed healer is motivated by his ego and as such must believe in its counsel. Central to his thought system is that we are victims of circumstances 'out there' in the world. What the unhealed healer believes about himself he will also believe about his client and thus reinforce his client's consciousness. As the whole aim of true healing is to undo the client's belief that circumstances and people can harm him, the unhealed healer only makes the client's illusion stronger.

5b. The Healed Healer: 'There are no victims. We all choose the events in our lives and how we want to react to them.'

> *It is impossible that the Son of God be merely driven by events outside of him. It is impossible that happenings that come to him were not his choice. His power of decision is the determiner of every situation in which he seems to find himself by chance or accident.*
>
> (T418; T-21.II.3:1-3)

The healed healer is aware that we all write the scripts of our lives, even though few of us are consciously aware of this or want to believe it. Our first choice was to be born on this planet because we believed happiness lay outside ourself. We all hope to find peace and happiness in the forms of this world. All that occurs in our lives is not by accident, for on some level we have chosen it.

When a particular event occurs, it is neutral in itself. We then choose how to see it, either through the eyes of the ego or those of the Holy Spirit. Our ego will either be attracted or repelled by the event, whilst the Holy Spirit will see it as another opportunity to learn forgiveness and move closer to God. It is not, however, a healing approach if, when someone shares with you some pain they are experiencing, you begin telling them that they have created this for themself and their pain is only due to separation from God. If you open to the Holy Spirit, He will guide you to be with the person where they believe they are and to work with correcting the error on the level where it is thought to be.

Jesus states: 'I was a man who remembered spirit and its knowledge. As a man I did not attempt to counteract error with knowledge, but to correct error from the bottom up.' (T39; T-3.IV.7:3-4) Thus Jesus met people on their own level and listened to their problems, even though he knew they were all illusory. He spoke to them in parables so that they could understand something of his truth.

Healing, like forgiveness and prayer, is a process. If a client is in great distress because their child has been raped and murdered, the process of healing will normally be a long one. The lesson in forgiveness is obviously powerful and must proceed in stages. Hopefully, the time will come when the client can perceive the fear in the murderer as the same fear he himself carries and that both need to open to receiving God's love. As he learns to forgive the murderer, so he learns to forgive himself and take another step on the path back to God.

Many of us believe that our problems originate in our early upbringing and the way we were treated by our mother or father. At the end of the healing journey, we will come to realise that all our problems stem from our fearful concept of our Parent in Heaven. When we at last heal this misperception and discover the totally loving and accepting Father waiting for us all, the need for healers will disappear.

6a. The Unhealed Healer: 'I have pity for the pain you are suffering.'

> *To empathise does not mean to join in suffering, for that is what you must refuse to understand. That is the ego's interpretation of empathy, and is always used to form a special relationship in which suffering is shared . . . The clearest proof that empathy as the ego uses it is destructive lies in the fact that it is applied only to certain types of problems and in certain people. These it selects out, and joins with. And it never joins except to strengthen itself.*
>
> (T307; T-16.I.1:1-2, 2:1-3)

The moment we take sides in any situation, the ego is in control. Victims and victimisers are both in a state of fear and both are asking for love. To empathise with the victim consciousness in another is to reinforce it in yourself as well. The client will feel justified in feeling a victim if pity or sympathy is shown by the therapist and the opportunity to forgive will be lost. Now the focus will shift to 'forgiving' the enemy 'out there' in the world — what Jesus calls 'forgiveness-to-destroy'.

Driven by the wrong motives and relying on his own ego strength, the unhealed healer often suffers from exhaustion or burnout. Some of the main reasons for this are:

- Attachment to results.
- Thinking that he is the healer.
- Believing the client has no inner strength of his own and is therefore reliant on the healer.
- Finding it hard to forgive himself for his own imperfections and judgements because of the superior position he puts himself in.
- Needing to be needed.
- Not stating his own needs.
- Difficulty in saying no to people's requests.
- Trying to heal the problem at the symptom level — 'out there' in the world.
- Forgetting to turn to the Holy Spirit for help.

6b. The Healed Healer: 'I acknowledge your pain and I empathise with the strength in you. My loving presence reminds you that the light of Christ is within you and that you can choose again.'

> *Yet of this you may be sure; if you will merely sit quietly by and let the Holy Spirit relate through you, you will empathise with strength, and will gain in strength and not weakness.*

$$\text{(T307; T-16.I.2:7)}$$

The healed healer works on two levels. He accepts the client where he is in his process but knows that he is not the ego that the client believes himself to be. As the healer recognises the Holy Spirit in himself, he must also see it in his client and this is what he empathises with. The healer does not commiserate with his client. The healer does not try to rationalise with the client or persuade him to change his mind about having chosen sickness. The client is unaware that he has chosen sickness and believes that he is a victim of his body's weakness.

On this issue the Course comments: 'They have no idea how insane this concept is. If they even suspected it, they would be healed, yet they suspect nothing. To them the separation is quite real.' (M18; M-5.III.1:10-12) This quotation is taken from a section in the Manual for Teachers entitled 'The function of the teacher of God'. We are reminded here that it is the peaceful, loving and accepting presence of a teacher of God which can provide the opportunity for the client to change his mind and choose forgiveness instead of attack.

The client is aware on some level that his pain does not disturb the healer. He is aware that the healer is seeing something else in him, other than his ego. It is the presence of the healed healer which gives the client an opportunity to know himself in another light, to let go of the past and open himself up to his true reality.

The only meaningful contribution the healer can make is to present an example of one whose direction has been changed for him, and who no longer believes in nightmares of any kind. The light in his mind will therefore answer the questioner, who must decide with God that there is light because he sees it.

(T160; T-9.V.7:4-5)

The healer's true function is to act as a reminder of another way of being, providing the client with an example of someone who believes in the reality of the Holy Spirit and not the ego. It is not the techniques the healer uses which bring about healing. As quoted earlier, 'It is not their hands that heal. It is not their voice that speaks the word of God. They merely give what has been given them.' (M18; M-5.III.2:8-10)

The Bible tells us that Jesus used his hands to heal and even his own spittle. He knew, however, that the people associated the laying on of hands with healing and believed that spittle contained healing power. He conformed to their needs and expectations by using their belief systems for their benefit. But it was his loving and gentle presence that reminded them they could choose to forgive and regain peace of mind instead of listening to the ego's counsel of separation, attack and sickness. Nor would the apparent severity of an illness concern Jesus, for he knew that all illness served the same purpose of making the ego's thought system real. If Jesus had thought that some diseases were more difficult to heal than others, he would be agreeing with the ego that there is a hierarchy of problems in this world. (See 'The Laws of Chaos' in Chapter 23 of the Text)

In every situation where Jesus was asked for healing, irrespective of the seeming seriousness of the disease, he would know he had only one task to perform — to dispel the illusion in the sick person's mind that he is separate from God and to show him that God still loves him and he is still as God created him.

As we tread the path of forgiveness, the light of the Holy Spirit will light up our mind as it did with Jesus and we shall extend it into the minds of others. It is that light, if it is accepted, that will heal others. When the ego is gone, only the Holy Spirit will remain in our mind to bless all whom we meet. The function of the decision maker will also disappear and we shall be guided moment by moment in what to say and do. The effort and confusion of choice will be replaced by the peace, joy and certainty of God and we shall know that we have been healed.

Forget not that the healing of God's Son is all the world is for. That is the only purpose the Holy Spirit sees in it, and thus the only one it has.

(T476; T-24.VI.4:1-2)

Appendices

- A Summary of *A Course in Miracles*.

- Chart of Key Concepts in *A Course in Miracles*.

- Recommended Books and Tapes on *A Course in Miracles*.

- Mail Order Distributors of *A Course in Miracles* and Related Materials.

- *A Course in Miracles,* Second Edition.

A Summary of
A Course in Miracles

'You may be surprised to hear how very different is reality from what you see.' (T348; T-18.I.5:1)[8] Our senses report to us a seemingly real and substantial world. The Course informs us, however, that we spend all our sleeping and waking time in a dream of seeming separation from God. Our true nature is still spirit, as God created us, and will be eternally. God is described as perfect, limitless, formless, eternal and changeless and so therefore His Creation, the Christ or Sonship, must also be. Nothing in our universe can be described by any of these words and therefore it cannot have been created by God. We are ideas in the mind of God and as ideas we cannot leave the mind of God. This perfect unity of God and Christ is Heaven and nothing can threaten this.

For reasons we cannot understand, a thought of separation from God, which the Course calls the ego, entered the collective mind of the Sonship. This idea, at which we 'forgot to laugh', stated that we could take the place of God and become the Creator. God's answer to this was the creation of the Holy Spirit in our mind to correct this 'tiny mad idea' of separation.

Choosing not to listen to the Voice for God, we experienced an overwhelming sense of sin at what we thought we had accomplished. From this act of sin came guilt and the fear of God's punishment. Our minds became split into the wrong mind of the ego, the right mind of the Holy Spirit and the sleeping Son of God (the decision maker) who has now to decide who to listen to. The ego part

---

[8] This summary, together with the chart on the following page, have been inspired by ideas contained in *Awaken from the Dream* by Gloria and Kenneth Wapnick. (See Recommended Books & Tapes)

Summary Chart of *A Course in Miracles*

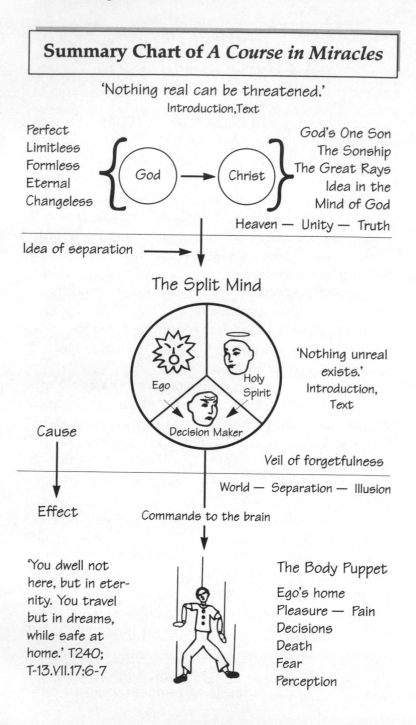

'Nothing real can be threatened.'
Introduction, Text

Perfect
Limitless
Formless
Eternal
Changeless

{ God → Christ }

God's One Son
The Sonship
The Great Rays
Idea in the
Mind of God

Heaven — Unity — Truth

Idea of separation ⟶

The Split Mind

Ego
Holy Spirit
Decision Maker

'Nothing unreal exists.'
Introduction, Text

Cause

Veil of forgetfulness

World — Separation — Illusion

Effect

Commands to the brain

'You dwell not here, but in eternity. You travel but in dreams, while safe at home.' T240; T-13.VII.17:6-7

The Body Puppet

Ego's home
Pleasure — Pain
Decisions
Death
Fear
Perception

counsels us that we cannot survive the avenging anger of God as represented by the presence of the Holy Spirit in our mind. Out of fear we listen to and identify with the ego's counsel and project the thought of separation out of our mind as an image. This image is the physical universe where we can now hide from God's anger and our guilt.

A veil of forgetfulness falls over our decision and this illusory world appears very real to us. Yet we are still safe in heaven although lost in our dream of exile. So powerful is this illusion that we could not awaken without the help of the Holy Spirit. Our body now seems a reality and not spirit which vision would reveal to us. The ego teaches us to deny our guilt and project it onto others. Our guilt (self-hate) now seems to be created by people and circumstances outside ourselves. We now feel justified in feeling anger towards others and attack in self-defence becomes a necessity (special hate relationships). Feeling a great lack within us, the ego counsels us to find people who can fulfil our imagined needs — security, sex, money, career etc (special love relationships).

To awaken from this dream and regain our lost vision, we need to undo our belief in separation from God. The Holy Spirit's plan for our awakening is called the Atonement (correction of perception). We begin to learn that the world is but a neutral mirror to the beliefs in our mind. No person or event has the power to give or take our peace from us. When we get disturbed about someone or something 'out there' in the world, we are only seeing a projection of some part of our mind that is not forgiven.

If we can have the 'little willingness' to allow the Holy Spirit's counsel of forgiveness to enter our mind, we can begin the journey of undoing separation by joining with others. We forgive by first removing our projections from the world and then bringing them back to our mind where they originated. Now we have the opportunity to heal our mind by ceasing to judge its ego content. It is our self-judgement that prevents our mind being healed by the Holy Spirit. Guilt demands punishment, not healing.

As we learn to stop judging ourselves, we allow the ever-present love of the Holy Spirit to shine away the clouds of guilt in our mind. This shift of perception, from the ego's world of separation and attack to the Holy Spirit's counsel of joining and forgiveness, is called a miracle. As we practise forgiveness in our relationships, we start to undo the guilt which covers the memory of God's love in our mind. We begin to see that we have not been running away from God's anger, but from God's love. To allow the awareness of God's love back into our mind will cause our ego to disappear, and this is our greatest fear.

Relationships become classrooms in which we learn to forgive ourselves by forgiving others (holy relationships). Jesus is the greatest example to us in teaching this lesson of forgiveness. Increasingly we realise that when people attack us through fear, they are really asking for our love. Thus we begin to allow the Holy Spirit to transform our world from the prison of the ego to a teaching device that will awaken us from the dream of separation and allow us to enter the real world of vision.

With the reawakening in our mind of the knowledge of who we really are, we will walk this world in complete peace, with an inner joy that nothing can take from us. We will now perceive everyone as our brothers and sisters whose reality is eternal spirit and to whom we extend the love of the Holy Spirit.

Key Concepts in *A Course in Miracles*

Heaven
The perfect unity of God and Christ

• Christ • Extension • Knowledge
• Spirit • One Mind • Will
• Love • Life • Eternity

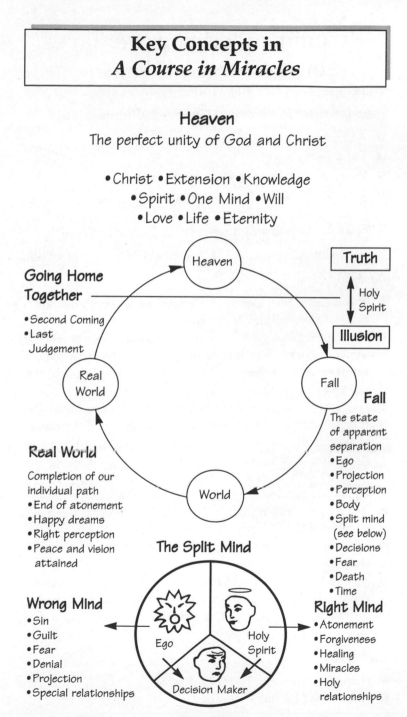

Heaven

Truth

Holy Spirit

Illusion

Going Home Together

• Second Coming
• Last Judgement

Real World

Fall

Fall

The state of apparent separation
• Ego
• Projection
• Perception
• Body
• Split mind (see below)
• Decisions
• Fear
• Death
• Time

Real World

Completion of our individual path
• End of atonement
• Happy dreams
• Right perception
• Peace and vision attained

World

The Split Mind

Ego

Holy Spirit

Decision Maker

Wrong Mind
• Sin
• Guilt
• Fear
• Denial
• Projection
• Special relationships

Right Mind
• Atonement
• Forgiveness
• Healing
• Miracles
• Holy relationships

Recommended Books & Tapes
on *A Course in Miracles*

Foundation for Inner Peace. Tiburon, California

- *A Course in Miracles.*
- *The Song of Prayer.*
- *Psychotherapy: Purpose, Process and Practice.*
- *The Gifts of God. The inspired poetry of Helen Schucman.*

Selected books and audio tapes by Dr Kenneth Wapnick

Published by the Foundation for A Course in Miracles, New York.

Books:

- *A Talk Given on A Course in Miracles.* An in-depth introduction to the principles of *A Course in Miracles.*
- *Christian Psychology in A Course in Miracles.* Focuses on the dynamics of the ego, its undoing through the Holy Spirit's forgiveness, and the role these themes have played in traditional Christianity.
- *Forgiveness and Jesus.* Also published by Arkana under the title *The Meaning of Forgiveness.* Addresses the misunderstandings of traditional Christianity, separating these out from the Course, and discusses the applications of the Course's principles to the major issues of our lives, such as injustice, anger, sickness, sexuality and money.
- *Absence From Felicity.* The story of Helen Schucman and her scribing of the Course.
- *Glossary — Index for A Course in Miracles.* A study guide for students of the Course.
- *Awaken From the Dream.* Written with Gloria Wapnick. A new presentation of the basic ideas of the Course and offering a different approach to the Course's metaphysical teaching of 'not making the error real'.

Tape Sets:

- *Healing the Unhealed Healer* — 8 tapes
- *Sickness and Healing* — 7 tapes

- *The Song of Prayer* — 9 tapes giving a line by line explanation of this pamphlet.
- *The Simplicity of Salvation* — 8 tapes presenting an in-depth summary of the principles of the Course.

Kenneth and Gloria Wapnick have an extensive number of books and tape sets available — I have mentioned only a few. I consider their publications to be the most authoritative on the subject of the Course.

Music

Songs From the Heart by Susan McCullen. From Songs of the Heart, 510 West Summit, Ann Arbor, MI 48103, USA. A beautiful tape of music and songs based on the Course's teachings.

Videos

The Story of A Course in Miracles. Foundation for Inner Peace, Tiburon, California. The first half of this two-and-a-half-hour documentary, *The Forgotten Song,* tells the story of how the Course came into existence. *The Song Remembered,* the second half of the film, contains first hand accounts of 27 students of the Course who tell what the material means to them, and how it has affected their lives.

Other Related Material

- *A Course in Miracles* along with the *Song of Prayer* and *Psychotherapy* pamphlets are available on computer diskettes. Center Link Information Services Inc., 3 Miller Road, Putnam Valley, New York 10579, USA. Tel/Fax 914-528-7617.
- *A Course in Miracles* on audio tape. Foundation for Inner Peace, Tiburon, California. Comprises 42 C90 audio cassettes containing the complete Course.
- *A Course in Miracles Workbook Lesson Cards.* Foundation for Inner Peace, Tiburon, California. All 365 Workbook Lessons reproduced on thick cards, enabling easy carrying of current Lessons.

Mail Order Distributors
of *A Course in Miracles* and related materials

USA

Foundation for *A Course in Miracles*
Conference and Retreat Center, 1275 Tennanah Lake Road, Roscoe, NewYork 12776-5905. Tel: (607) 498-4116. Fax: (607) 498-5325. Kenneth and Gloria Wapnick produce *The Lighthouse* newsletter which contains ordering information for all their books and tapes plus publications of The Foundation for Inner Peace. Details of the Center's workshops, seminars and academy programme are also included.

Miracle Distribution Center
1141 East Ash Avenue, Fullerton, California 92631. Toll Free Ordering: 1-800 359 ACIM. General information: Tel: (714) 738-8380. They produce a newsletter, *The Holy Encounter*, a comprehensive mail order catalogue, and keep a world-wide list of *A Course in Miracles* study groups.

Miracles Community Network
PO Box 418, Santa Fe, New Mexico 87504-0418. They produce a comprehensive mail order catalogue.

The above US distributors accept VISA payments.

Australia

Graham Watts
2/1 Kinsale Crescent, Mont Albert, Vic 3129. Tel: (03) 890 1864.

UK & Europe

Phoenix Mail Order
The Park, Findhorn, Forres IV36 0TZ, Scotland. Tel: 0309 691074. Fax: 0309 690933. *A Course in Miracles* and related books and videos. Information available on request.

A Course in Miracles, Second Edition

The second edition of *A Course in Miracles* has been newly type-set with the addition of line, paragraph and section numbers. A few pages of previously omitted material has also been included. This new material does not add any new concepts but expands upon the existing content of the Course. This work has added additional pages to the Course, resulting in the two editions having different page numbers.

The following notation, as used in the forthcoming Concordance on the Course, is used in this book to identify the line references in the second edition of the Course.

Examples of this notation:

T-10.VI.3:4

- Sentence
- Paragraph
- Section
- Chapter
- Text

W-pI.8.6:4

- Sentence
- Paragraph
- Lesson
- Part I
- Workbook

M-1.3:4-6

- Sentences
- Paragraph
- Question
- Manual

C-2.4:5

- Sentence
- Paragraph
- Term
- Clarification of terms

A Cross Reference Chart enabling readers to go back and forth between the first and second editions is available free of charge from the Foundation for Inner Peace Inc., P.O. Box 1104, Glen Ellen, California 95442, USA. Please enclose money to cover postage and handling.

The second editions of *Psychotherapy: Purpose, Process and Practice* and *The Song of Prayer* have now been published and have section, chapter, paragraph and line numbers inserted.

Michael and Salice Dawson are now living in Australia, where they continue to give talks, seminars and workshops on *A Course in Miracles*. If you would like information about their programmes, please write to them care of Findhorn Press, The Park, Findhorn, Forres IV36 0TZ, Moray, Scotland.